Drive through Russia?

Impossible!

DRIVE
THROUGH
RUSSIA?

IMPOSSIBLE!

Allen L. Johnson

VANTAGE PRESS
New York / Washington / Atlanta
Los Angeles / Chicago

FIRST EDITION

Published by Vantage Press, Inc.
516 West 34th Street, New York, New York 10001

Manufactured in the United States of America
ISBN: 0-533-06695-6

Library of Congress Catalog Card No.: 85-90204

To Gloria, my wife, typist, editor,
and traveling companion

Contents

Preface

After undertaking a trip through the western part of the Soviet Union by automobile, I felt the urge to document my experiences so that others who are considering a similar trip can benefit from my mistakes. I hope to provide the answers to some of the practical questions about driving through the Soviet Union that I searched for unsuccessfully before my trip. I'd like to dispel some of the fears and the mystique surrounding such a trip and suggest ways of making better preparations for what was a very interesting, informative, and rewarding adventure.

In the book's title I've used *Russia* in the casual and inaccurate way it is often used in conversation. The proper term is the Union of Soviet Socialist Republics. But when I told people that my wife and I planned to drive from Leningrad down to the Black Sea, the reply was, "Drive through Russia? Impossible!" In the book, I attempt to use the "Soviet Union" when I am referring to the collective republics and "Russia" when I mean just the Russian republic.

After I returned from the Soviet Union, I happened upon a book Will Rogers wrote about his adventures there in the 1920s. To my surprise, fifty-five years later, I ran into the same problems he did. The method Will Rogers used to tell his story was like that used by the prisoner in the courtroom when some wise, old, good-natured judge who wanted to get at the facts asked, "Will you please tell the court, in your own way and your own language, exactly what happened on the entire night of June the twelfth?"

Well, Your Honor, my wife and I were sitting in Row 19 of this Pan American jet when. . . .

Drive through Russia?

Impossible!

Chapter 1
Introduction

Our first view of the Soviet Union came on a cold November day in 1974, when our Pan Am 707 broke through the thick, gray clouds, and touched down at Moscow's Sheremetyevo Airport. There was a light powder of snow on the fields and in the beautiful birch forest surrounding the airport. To our surprise, the countryside, just a few miles from this capital city of 8 million people, had a rural appearance.

I had been invited to Moscow to present a technical paper at a scientific meeting being held at the Ismiran Technical Institute, just outside Moscow. To share the adventure, I had brought my wife, Gloria, my cousin Pat, and her husband, Bob. We spent eight days in Moscow attending the meeting and then flew to Kiev, Yalta, and Leningrad for sightseeing.

"Gee! Wouldn't it be fun to drive between the cities rather than fly?" suggested Pat.

"Impossible!" replied Intourist, the official Soviet tourist organization.

Years later, as we sat around the crackling fireplace at Pat and Bob's farm in northern Illinois and reminisced about our Russian adventure, the idea of touring the Soviet Union again at a leisurely pace where we could see the rural side of Soviet life kept coming up.

"I'd like to see one of their collective farms," said Bob.

"I'm interested in the small-village life," said Pat.

"I'd like to meet some of their cats," mused Gloria as she gently stroked the calico fur of Pat's barn cat.

I checked with Tasha, our travel agent, about an auto tour of the Soviet Union.

"Impossible," she said, "but I can get you on a nice sixteen-day bus tour with a native-speaking guide."

Because of my training as an engineer and my twenty years of experience with research and development, I take the word *impossible* as a personal challenge. To me it means the solution is not obvious, but will require further study.

In 1978 I had a trip to Norway for a technical meeting and decided to pursue the Russian idea a little further. I stopped by the Aeroflot (official Russian airlines) office in Oslo and asked where I could get information about driving through the Soviet Union.

"Impossible!" said the Aeroflot agent.

"I read in a travel magazine where certain roads are now open to foreigners," I said.

"Very difficult," said the agent. "Must be arranged long in advance. Why don't you fly? We have several nice accompanied tours."

"No. I want to drive," I insisted.

"Maybe you should talk to Intourist. They have an office down the street."

I wasn't sure if she was just trying to get rid of me or not, but I walked down to the Intourist office. I told the Intourist agent about my idea of driving through the Soviet Union and waited for the inevitable "Impossible!"

"Very exciting idea," he commented. "You will have a very interesting trip," he said as he dug out a booklet titled *Motor Tours of the Soviet Union*.

The booklet asked: "Can you see much from a moving train or airliner? A car has a definite advantage because it gives you a close-up view of the country, its town and villages, its beauty spots and wildlife preserves. Last but not least, it is possible to see the people at work and at leisure."

This was the "gotcha" for us. Gloria and I love seeing strange, exotic lands, but most of all, we enjoy meeting the people. In small American towns, people are more apt to stop and talk to you than in the big cities. That appears to be a universal characteristic of small-town people. The opportunity to rub shoulders with the small-town Soviet citizen was too good to ignore.

The winter of 1978, Gloria and I made our decision to go back to the Soviet Union and started planning our "impossible" adventure. I contacted Pat and Bob to see if they wanted to return with us.

"Love to," said Pat, "but right now we've got some other priorities that are higher than a trip to Russia."

So Gloria and I sat down and started laying out our itinerary. If we are going to be on our own in the Russian countryside, it would be important to be able to speak the language. We arranged to take a year of Russian at our local university. Then we contacted a tutor to sharpen us up on speaking and comprehension.

Our tutor, Mrs. Chazin, is a sparkling little silver-haired lady who immigrated to this country from the Ukraine just prior to the Russian Revolution and studied at Columbia University. Currently she is teaching in the public-school system as a substitute teacher. Her subjects include Russian, English, sign language, and about anything else except math. She has a warm, supportive method of teaching that never embarrasses a student or leaves him or her afraid to try a new word or phrase. She employs unorthodox approaches to get her point across. One night when she was teaching us some new sounds, she worked on the word *borsch* (beet soup). She wasn't pleased with our pronounciation as we repeated the word. She jumped up from the table we were using as a desk and hustled off to her kitchen. She returned a minute later with a bowl of borsch for each of us.

"Eat," she said. "It is very delicious and very healthful. It's borsch."

When we had eaten our borsch she said, "Now, repeat, *borsch. . . .*"

"Borsch."

"That's good," she said. "Now you are learning."

After two years of study with our tutor, we could recite Pushkin's poem "Farewell to the Black Sea" and felt confident about communicating in Russian. We had mastered the language well enough to ask for the nearest gas station, the road to Suzdal, and where to get the best Ukrainian food in Kiev.

As we were poring over the Intourist brochures, Fodor's Russian travel book, and Soviet literature, our route slowly took shape. Since it would be difficult to rent a car in one Soviet city and drop it at another destination, we decided to rent a car in Denmark for the entire tour. There was also discount air fare (Apex) to Copenhagen. We planned to drive through Sweden and Finland, entering the Soviet Union near Leningrad. To avoid backtracking, we decided to drive down to Moscow and on to Odessa, by the Black Sea. We would exit through Hungary and return to Copenhagen through Austria and Germany. The trip would cover about 6,000 miles.

During early 1981, Gloria and I contacted our travel agent and set the wheels in motion. We submitted a detailed itinerary specifying what city we would like to visit each day. Our travel agent contacted Shipka Agency in Cleveland, which is accredited with Intourist. Shipka then submitted our itinerary to Intourist. It took about five or six weeks for Intourist to digest our itinerary and ask Shipka for a $997 payment for the nineteen nights we would be in the Soviet Union. Intourist approved our itinerary with only minor changes.

While we were waiting for our itinerary to be approved, we got our airline reservations and my international driver's license, checked our passports, and firmed up the rental-car reservation.

Once our hotels were booked and paid for, we were allowed to submit passports with the visa request. In accordance with the Russian Embassy's reputation for keeping tourists off balance, the visas came back the day before our scheduled departure.

As the magic departure day approached, we gathered the essentials for the trip: running shoes, washcloths, vitamin C, ten packages of gum, twenty rolls of film, a sewing kit, Woolite, Pepto-Bismol, a hair dryer (with European adapter), et cetera. The night before we left, we had our last session with our Russian tutor. She fed us piroshki (dumplings with potatoes, cheese, or fruit inside) and shed a few tears as she wished us "*Shchastlivogo puti*" (Happy Journey).

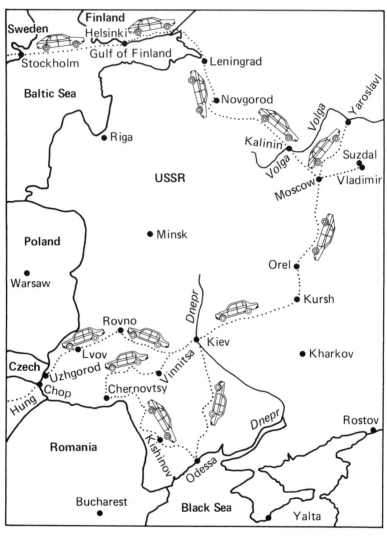

From Denmark we drove across Sweden and Finland, entering the Soviet Union near Leningrad. Four thousand miles later, we left the Soviet Union and entered Hungary.

Chapter 2
Departure: "Should be Able to Knock Ninety Seconds off That Time"

Our departure was uneventful except for the suicidal New York taxi ride. Our U.S. Air flight arrived late in New York, and we had only fifty-five minutes to cross from LaGuardia Airport to Kennedy International Airport to make our 6:00 P.M. departure. We entered the Friday-evening traffic jam with our kamikaze taxi driver screaming out of LaGuardia, switching lanes every ten seconds to get through the rush-hour traffic. After a fifteen-mile, heart-stopping ride, we arrived at Kennedy with a few minutes to spare. The taxi driver was not especially pleased with his time and wanted to try it again.

"Should be able to knock ninety seconds off that time," he lamented as I handed him a well-deserved tip.

We arrived at Copenhagen's International Airport on a clear, crisp Saturday morning after a comfortable Boeing 747 flight. The weather was sunny and eighteen degrees Celsius (fifty-nine degrees Fahrenheit). We checked on our rental car to see that all the paperwork was in order. Taking a western car into the Soviet Union is not without its difficulties. The clerk was halfway through filling out the rental contract when he casually asked where we planned to go for our vacation.

"Russia," I offered.

"Russia!" he repeated with a wide-eyed expression. "The last Americans who took one of our cars to Russia were arrested and thrown into prison. The Russians beat them and finally sent them back to America on an airplane. Our car is still sitting in Russia."

He dramatically tore our rental contract in a thousand pieces.

"Where can we find a car agency that rents cars to take into Russia?"

"Try Pitzner down the street," he suggested.

"I'd like to rent a car and drive it to Russia," I told the blue-eyed blonde attendant at Pitzner Auto.

"How long would you like the car for?" she asked.

"A month," I replied.

"No problem," she assured me. "We'll take care of all the paperwork, registration, insurance forms, and a spare-parts kit."

As we walked outside to pick up our car, Gloria commented, "She doesn't care if the Russians arrest us, throw us in jail, and beat us."

The attendant emerged from the underground garage with our brand-new Opel Kadett (seven kilometers on it) gassed up and ready to go. She showed me a parts kit with fan belts, spark plugs, fuses, lamps, and points.

Gloria and I drove back to our hotel and caught up on our sleep for the rest of the day. The six-hour time difference and all-night flight had left us a little limp. On Sunday morning, we hopped in our shiny, new, red Opel Kadett and set off for Sweden. A short one-hour drive to Helsingor and a twenty-minute ferry ride put us at Helsingborg, Sweden.

We drove off the ferry and got our first glimpse of the "Swedish illness," as our Danish friends call it. In Sweden, the law requires that you drive with headlights on day or night. I'm not sure if it is the safety lobby or the headlight lobby that got that law passed. It does increase visibility of an oncoming car, but I could never remember to turn the lights off when I got out of the car.

In Nassjo, Sweden, we visited my cousin Asta. She is a bubbly lady in her sixties, married to a retired florist, Gunar.

We rented an Opel Kadett in Copenhagen and drove it 4,000 miles through the Soviet Union and back to Denmark without any mechanical problems.

They rent a cozy, four-room apartment on the edge of a lake just a block from the center of town. Her apartment is decorated with needlework tapestries, family photos, and fresh flowers. We talked about my grandmother (Asta's aunt), and Asta took us to see where my grandmother had been born. After the drive, she invited us to have coffee. She served eight different breads and cakes that she had baked. I studied for a moment to decide which to try.

"You must take one of each," Asta informed me. "It's the custom in Smoland [south central Sweden]."

With eight cakes and a couple of cups of strong Swedish coffee, we were awake until after midnight. I used the time to read about the Russian traffic regulations, and Gloria started translating the Swedish knitting books she had bought.

9

The next day, we drove to Stockholm and caught the Finnish ferry for Helsinki. We rode in a ten-story–high ship, the *Finlandia*, a brand-new ship on the Silja line. Our spacious cabin on number 6 deck featured a large picture window. No more portholes! Once on board, I realized how different the Finnish language was from any other we had encountered. Common expressions like "yes" (*kylla*), "no" (*ei*), and "good morning" (*hyvaa huomenta*) bore no resemblance to any language that I know. Even the universal word *telephone* is not recognizable in Finland. It is *puhelin*. To confuse the issue even more, the country isn't even called Finland. In Finnish it's Suomi. Why can't a country be called what the natives call it? Suomi is a fine name for a country. If Mrs. Logan, my fifth-grade geography teacher, had told me that Suomi was a beautiful, wooded country with 4.6 million people in northern Europe, I would have taken the statement at face value.

Gloria and I stood on deck for a couple of hours as the ship sailed out the coastal channel to the Gulf of Finland. After we had been sailing two hours, the Swedish coastal islands were still in view, often within a few hundred meters of the ship. What a beautiful, but dangerous channel! We had supper in the main dining room and sat mesmerized by the flashing beacons from nearby lighthouses. After supper, we danced to a five-piece Finnish band on a ten-by-ten–foot dance floor near a two-story–high picture window at the front of the boat. The view was breathtaking, and the band had a nice beat. They played old Finnish favorites like "Deep Purple," "The Pennsylvania Polka," and "Tiny Bubbles."

About 10:00 P.M., the sky turned a rosy red as the sun tried to set. At sixty degrees north latitude, the sun is up about twenty hours a day in June. I fell asleep at midnight with the bright twilight still shining in the cabin. At 3:00 A.M., sunrise awakened me.

At 9:00 A.M., the ferry docked in Helsinki. After a brief,

courteous customs and passport check, Gloria and I left for the hotel. We had asked our travel agent to book a moderately priced hotel in the center of the city.

"Where is the Dipoli Hotel?" I asked the purser.

"In Espo."

"Where's Espo?"

"About twelve kilometers west of Helsinki."

We found the highway and headed west. About twenty kilometers from Helsinki, there were still signs designating the way to Espo Center. I decided to revert to the old American fail-safe navigation procedure and stopped at the nearest gas station for directions.

The beautiful, blue-eyed, blonde attendant did not speak a word of English and had never heard of the Dipoli Hotel. She applied a Finnish navigation trick and got out the telephone book. Finnish phone books have detailed maps that show the shops and hotels in addition to other points of interest. We found the Dipoli Hotel, but couldn't relate where it was with where we were. I produced my large-scale map of Finland and finally matched up the telephone map and mine. In another twenty minutes, Gloria and I arrived at the luxurious Dipoli Hotel and Sports Complex. It's located on a bay eight or nine miles west of Helsinki. It consists of a beautiful hotel, sports arena, sailing area, convention center, and restaurant.

"Maybe this won't be so bad," I told Gloria and went into the spacious lobby to register.

"Room for Mr. and Mrs. Johnson, please."

"There must be a mistake," the room clerk replied. "We are booked up."

How quickly panic strikes when a room clerk cuts you down. I fumbled for my reservation confirmation.

"We have confirmed reservations," I said as I handed him the copy of the travel agent's deposit check. He picked up the telephone to check the reservations.

"Ah, yes," he said. "You are in our summer hotel up the road."

The "summer hotel" turned out to be a four-story dormitory for the nearby technical university. During the summer, it was turned into a youth hostel. We got a quiet dormitory room on the fourth floor. The room was identical to the one I shared at the University of Illinois in 1953. Even the furniture was the same—two single beds standing twelve inches off the floor, a desk, a bookcase, and one chair. The beds had plywood for springs and a two-inch–thick cotton mattress. The room made me nostalgic about my college days.

Before lunch, Gloria and I decided to drive down to Helsinki for a little sightseeing and shopping. Helsinki turned out to be a bright, cheerful city with enough old forts and museums and attractive shops to keep us busy for a week. After a whirlwind tour of the city, we drove back to the Dipoli.

In the evening, we got on our running gear and followed the path down to the lake. As we jogged around the lake, we encountered the damp, musty smell of the thick pine forest, interspersed with the sweet, fresh smell of the wildflowers that crowded the lake shore.

By suppertime, Gloria and I were both as hungry as bears. We found a small student café near our dormitory. The menu was written on a large blackboard in Finnish. When the waitress/cook asked what we wanted in Finnish, I knew we were in trouble. She was a college coed in Levis and a sweatshirt. Seeing our plight, she motioned us to come back to the kitchen, where she showed us what she had in the various pots and kettles. We chose a bubbling stew, which was delicious.

The next morning, Gloria and I woke early, full of anticipation, since this was the day we'd enter the Soviet Union and our impossible adventure would begin. We had a hearty breakfast of juice, hard-boiled eggs, cheese, rolls, yogurt, and tea. Not knowing what the food would be like in the Soviet Union, we took on enough calories to last us several days. We drove back through Helsinki and west through Finland. Before leaving Finland, we took certain precautions recommended in the tour books:

1. We filled the car with gas at $2.75 a gallon.
"Gasoline may be difficult to obtain in the Soviet Union."

—Soviet-tour book

2. We washed the car.
"It is illegal to drive a dirty car in the Soviet Union.

—*Driving Through the U.S.S.R.*

3. We took the windshield wipers off and put them under the front seat.
"Most Soviets take their windshield wipers off when they leave the car."

—Soviet-tour book

4. We bought a quart of oil in a reusable container.
"Oil is available at benzin stations in the Soviet Union, but you must bring your own container."

—Intourist guidebook

5. We got the car registration and insurance cards out and handy.
"Cars entering the Soviet Union must show international certificate of registration and insurance."

—Intourist guidebook

Chapter 3
The Soviet Border: "Good Trip!
I Should Go with You!"

As Gloria and I drove out of Finland, it was difficult to tell how close we were to the Soviet Union. The houses and farms spread right up to the border's edge. Suddenly there was a barrier and a guardhouse. The Finnish officer looked at our passports and raised the gate to let us through. A few hundred yards down the road, we stopped at the gate operated by two Soviet soldiers. They asked for our passports and studied them carefully for a moment before handing them back. They raised the gate and motioned for us to drive through.

"That was easier than I expected," Gloria commented.

The countryside looked much like that of Finland, with pine trees, rocky soil, and a two-lane blacktop road. However, we did notice that there were no houses or farms near the border. A mile or two into the Soviet Union, we came upon a sign warning of a stop ahead. The advertised stop was the customs checkpoint. We pulled off into an area that looked like a Howard Johnson's rest plaza located on any American turnpike. This was not a restaurant or comfort area. There were three separate lanes for buses, trucks, and cars. We queued up behind a dozen other cars from Finland, Sweden, and Germany. The agent took two cars at a time at the little custom house, one on each side. The routine was the same for each car:

• Surrender passport and visa.

- Remove all baggage from the car, place it on the table, and open it.
- Fill out the currency declaration form and vehicle registration form in duplicate.
- Surrender Intourist hotel vouchers.

We watched as three or four customs agents disassembled our car. All the seats came out, as well as the upholstery and spare tire. They probed into the gas tank with a long wire, in the doors, and down between the windows with a little mirror on a wire. One soldier slid under the car and pounded on the bottom side while the second felt the top of the floor to see if there were any secret compartments.

As we watched, I noticed a gigantic German shepherd lying in front of his doghouse, about twenty or thirty feet from the custom house. He got up and came over to smell my car. I thought he was going to take a bite out of one of the tires, but he just sniffed it. The customs agent in charge talked to him and pointed at his doghouse. The dog gave him a hurt look, as if to say, "I was just doing my job," and trotted back to his house. He lay down with his head on his paws and eyed us suspiciously as the soldier continued to inspect our car.

As the customs agents put our car back together, the young Soviet officer came over to see how we were faring with the currency declaration form. We had made no progress since the one he had given us was in German.

"I don't understand," I said. "Do you have one in English?"

He returned to the office and came back in a few minutes and asked if we spoke Russian.

"*Nemnogo* [A little]," I replied.

He rolled his eyes upward, giving us one of those "Why me?" expressions.

"We get very few English-speaking tourists through this

border," he explained in a combination of English and Russian. "Mostly French, Scandinavian, and German."

I realized we had reached a monumental milestone. Between his limited English and our limited Russian, I was actually conversing with a real Soviet in Russian and making myself understood. After we broke the ice, he became very chatty.

"Studied one year of English, know German and Finnish, but little English," he said. "Where are you going?"

"Leningrad, Moscow, Kiev, Odessa," I said.

"Good trip!" he acknowledged. "I should go with you! You put baggage back in car now."

"*Shchastlivogo puti,*" he called as Gloria and I drove off on our impossible adventure.

As we continued down the road, we encountered a huge forest of birch trees. These beautiful, white-barked trees brought back memories of scenes from *Dr. Zhivago*. We felt like stopping and wandering through the woods, but remembering how touchy the Soviets are about their border area, we decided to drive on. We saw stands of pine and spruce, but still no houses or farms.

About ten miles from the border, we passed a beautiful, clear stream. Two towheaded boys dropped their fishing poles to run up the bank and wave as we drove by. A mile farther, we drove by four young girls walking along the road. They had on black dresses with full white pinafore aprons. They wore white bouquets of ribbons in their hair. It was like a vision out of a Russian folk story. The girls waved and giggled as we drove by.

Now farms and small wooden houses began to appear along the road. It was still not heavily cultivated, like the Finnish countryside, but there were signs of life. We stopped at another checkpoint a few miles farther along while the guards checked the trunk of the car ahead of us, but they waved us on. In Vyborg, about forty miles from the border,

16

we stopped to change money, buy gas coupons, and exchange our hotel voucher. The Intourist agent read the itinerary.

"Very interesting. I should like to go with you maybe," was her comment.

The gas coupons cost about eighty-five cents per gallon, a bargain these days. We changed some dollars into rubles at an exchange rate of 73 rubles for 100 dollars or one ruble for about $1.33 in American money.

"Where are we staying in Leningrad?" I asked.

In the Soviet Union, you do not have a choice of hotels. You tell Intourist which city you wish to visit, and they tell you at which hotel you will stay.

"The Pribaltiskaya," she replied. "The newest hotel in Leningrad."

"And at what hotel in Novgorod?"

"Intourist in Leningrad will advise you of further reservations," she replied.

The average road in the Soviet Union is a two-lane cement or blacktop highway reminiscent of a secondary road in Illinois or Wisconsin.

In the Soviet Union, information seems to be at a premium. They dish it out a little at a time as if you might choke if they gave you the whole load. We set out for Leningrad, about 150 miles away. There was heavy traffic along the road—lots of trucks, buses, and a few cars. The road reminded me of a blacktop secondary road in Wisconsin. The countryside was rolling, green, forest-covered, and lightly populated. There is a 90 kilometer per hour (56 mph) speed limit in the country, but due to the turns, hills, and trucks, 45 or 50 mph is about all you can comfortably drive. There are a minimum of road signs, but the ones you see are the international type and easily understood. Local town signs are in the Russian Cyrillic alphabet. Those for the major cities, like Leningrad, are in both English and Russian.

About every twenty or thirty miles, there was a roadside rest stop. The rest stops had a graveled parking area and occasionally a bench or picnic table, depending on the level of activity of the local council. Often there was a concrete ramp to drive your car up so that you could change the oil or do other work under it. None of the rest stops was equipped with toilets or fresh water. Usually there was a stand of bushes nearby if you needed relief. Gloria and I stopped at several roadside parks and took pictures of the farms, fields, and countryside.

In one small town, an oncoming car flashed his lights at us. I quickly checked to see that the street wasn't a one-way and tried to figure out what he could have wanted. I watched in my rearview mirror as he stopped, turned around, and came up behind me. I thought it might be an unmarked police car, but still didn't know what I did or was doing wrong.

"You'd better stop and see what they want," said Gloria as the car went around me. I saw three youths inside.

One of them in the backseat held up some Russian rubles and yelled out the window, "Change money?"

The roadside stops are usually graveled areas devoid of toilets, drinking water, or tables. If the local council is active, there may be a bench to sit on and bushes for relief.

"*Nyet,*" I said and went on.

It's against the law to exchange money except at official government exchanges. The Soviet Union is quite firm on this point, and violators get a stiff jail sentence if they are caught. For major currency violations, the death sentence is authorized.

With American dollars, a Russian can buy liquor, cigarettes, and chocolates at the Beriozka store at a much lower price than they can buy such items in the local Soviet stores. After pursuing us for a few miles, the youths finally gave up, turned around and headed back to town.

"Navigating in Russia is a snap," I remarked to Gloria as we headed down the only paved road we'd seen for the past forty miles. About that time, we came upon Zelenogorsk, a small Russian town on the shore of the Baltic. We approached a major intersection of three roads. I glanced at the road sign showing the five-way intersection and was confused as to which road went to Leningrad.

"What did that sign say about Leningrad?" I asked Gloria.

"What sign?"

"The big green road sign we just passed."

"Oh. I didn't see a sign. I was watching a little yellow kitten climb a tree back there."

By that time, I was at the intersection and realized I wouldn't get a second chance at the sign. Traffic was coming from all five ways, and there was no hint which way went to Leningrad. I took a wild guess and picked the road that turned the least from our original direction.

"I would have taken the other road," said Gloria.

"Why?"

"Because the houses are prettier down that road," she replied logically.

We drove a few blocks, and doubt set in.

"I think we should turn around," said Gloria.

Checking the location of the sun, I had a sinking feeling we were headed west rather than south. About that time, we came upon the Baltic Sea.

"How come the Baltic is on your side?" asked Gloria.

"Because we're headed back to Finland," I growled as I pulled into a driveway to turn around. We headed back toward the center of town.

"Here comes a police car toward us," said Gloria pointing down the road at a black-and-white car approaching us. "I'll bet they arrest us and throw us in jail and beat us."

The police car went by slowly and continued down the

road. A few minutes later, as we approached the center of town, we encountered another police car.

"I'll bet they stop us and take all our luggage and send us home on an airplane," said Gloria.

The police slowed down and then continued on.

"There's the sign to Leningrad," I said with relief.

"What sign?" said Gloria, still watching the police.

We turned right at the five-way intersection and got back on the Leningrad road. As we picked our way through the rest of the town, Gloria commented, "I knew you'd find the way. I wasn't worried."

We made no further reference to the ease of navigation.

Chapter 4
Leningrad:
"It Is Not Necessary for You to Know"

In the cool of the evening, we entered Peter the Great's Venice of the North, Leningrad. It is a beautiful city of over 4 million people about 150 miles from the Finnish border. Almost 1 million of those people swarmed across the highway in front of our car in a mad dash to get home. They displayed infinite confidence in my driving ability while I tried to read the map, follow Gloria's directions, and avoid a collision with the other three lanes of traffic.

As we approached the center of the city, I pulled over frequently to check our progress. We stopped at the first corner and found no street signs on the side of the building. Back in traffic and down to the red light we drove. There was a street sign at that intersection, but it wasn't on the map. After four or five similar occurences, I was convinced the Russians didn't put signs on any streets named on the map.

Leningrad boasts of 68 rivers or canals, 110 islands, and 700 bridges. After crossing eight or ten bridges, we began to get an inkling of where we were. If we could find the right island out of those 110, we would be all set. After a frustrating hour of touring, we finally achieved that goal. Now if we drove west and didn't cross any more bridges, we should see a fifteen-story building near the edge of the city. Sure enough. We fell in behind the Number 18 bus and followed it right up to the hotel.

The Pribaltiskaya is a gigantic building that could have been used for a set in *King Kong*. There is a huge central section with two massive wings filling up a reclaimed swamp along the shores of the Baltic Sea. The parking lot looked like it was designed to hold the Indy 500 crowd. It was empty except for six cars. Our car made the seventh as we pulled up near the steps. As we climbed the 150 steps to the entrance, Gloria commented, "This looks like where the virgins would be sacrificed."

We entered the huge doors and approached the counter, which extended 150 feet in front of us. I got the attention of one of the ladies behind the counter and presented our hotel vouchers.

"Individual tourist must go around the corner to the Intourist Service Bureau," she said.

Around the corner we went. We entered an auditorium-sized hall with twenty-two Intourist agents camped in the center and a magnificent stained-glass wall behind them. Each agent sat at a gigantic desk with an illuminated globe announcing her special function:

- Information
- Service
- Tickets
- Excursions
- Telephone calls
- Cashier
- Telegrams
- Future bookings
- Individual bookings

We approached the individual-bookings desk and gave the pretty, brunette Russian lady our vouchers. She filled out our room card and took our passports.

"You can get your passports tomorrow at the reception desk."

"Can you tell us which hotel we'll be staying at in the next city?"

She got out a stack of papers and leafed through them. "Ah," she said, "you will be at the Intourist hotel in Novgorod, the newest hotel in that city."

"Could you tell us the street address of the Intourist hotel?"

"It is not necessary for you to know. You just stop and ask when you get to Novgorod."

No need to argue; it was not necessary for us to know, and that was that. She looked over our planned stops.

"Very interesting itinerary. You should have a good trip," she said as she gave us our room card. "Your room is not ready yet; you'll have to wait a few minutes."

While we waited for our room, the Intourist agent related a brief history of this beautiful city. Leningrad is a relatively new city, by Russian standards, being conceived less than 300 years ago. When Peter the Great became Czar in 1682, he vowed to change Russia from a backward, medieval country to a great civilized nation. With the successful conclusion of the Northern War with Sweden, Peter the Great started to build a fortress on his newly won territory where the Neva River ran into the Gulf of Finland. His desire was to establish a year-round port with access to the Baltic—a "window to the West." Surveying the area, Peter picked Hare Island near the north bank of the river for his stronghold. The czar cut two strips of turf with a bayonet and laid one across the other. "Here," he said, "there shall be a town."

Peter supervised the work on the Peter and Paul Fortress from a wooden hut on a neighboring island. He went on to construct a port and build the town. As the town took shape, he came up with a bold plan to make the town the capital of Russia. He forbade the building of wooden houses and required people coming to the area to bring building stones with them. All ships docking at his port had to carry building stones as part of their cargo.

Carving a town out of the marshy wilderness was not an easy task. In 1705, Peter was almost drowned when a sudden flood occurred. As late as 1714, two sentries were eaten by wolves as they crossed the river near one of the palaces.

In 1712, Saint Petersburg was sufficiently finished to be officially proclaimed capital of the empire. At Peter's insistence, the nobility had palaces built in Saint Petersburg and every landowner in the country who had more than fifteen serf families was forced to build a house in the new capital.

Peter started building the first Winter Palace for Saint Petersburg in 1711. Another palace was added in 1721, and then these were replaced in 1754 with the first building of the current Winter Palace (the Hermitage). Peter the Great's gamble had paid off. A half-century after he stood on the bleak marsh on the shore of the Baltic, Catherine the Great was entertaining the heads of European royalty in a city that had taken its place among the great capitals of the world.

Saint Petersburg remained the capital of Russia for 150 years. In 1905, the first phase of the Russian Revolution began, when a huge workers' demonstration was fired upon by the Imperial Guard in Victory Square in front of the Winter Palace. In 1914, the city underwent a name change to a more Russian Petrograd. In 1917, the armed uprising of an army of workers, soldiers, and sailors gave power to the Soviets and permitted the formation of the first workers' and peasants' government under Lenin. The next year, the capital was moved back to Moscow. In 1924, the city underwent another name change to the current Leningrad.

During the Second World War, Leningrad was attacked

by the Nazis. Hitler expected to overrun the city in days or weeks. Nine hundred days later, the Russians fired a victory salute over Leningrad as the Nazi troops retreated, having never set foot in the city. However, the price was tremendous. Over 650,000 people died during the blockade of Leningrad, and more than 10,000 buildings were damaged by bombs and artillery fire.

The present-day city shows none of the war damage. The eighteenth-century palaces and churches have been restored, and a host of new twentieth-century hotels, offices, and apartment buildings have replaced those completely destroyed.

After a fifteen-minute wait, the Intourist agent got a phone call saying our room was ready.

The room was modern and well decorated, with the ever-present twin beds. It overlooked the Baltic Sea and contained a television, radio, and writing desk. There was a modern tub, a shower, and all the comforts of home. Our first priority was supper, since it had been twelve hours since breakfast in Finland. We selected one of the hotel's five restaurants, the Neva, because it advertised specialties of Russian Cuisine. Our waitress, Sasha, a pretty, blond girl about twenty years old, had expressive dark-blue eyes that twinkled as she welcomed us. She wore a short black dress with a dainty, embroidered white apron. She had a fair command of English, but agreed to patronize us and let us try our feeble Russian while ordering.

"My wife will have chicken Kiev, and I'll have the filet peasant style, with white wine, cucumber salad, and black bread."

"Just wine to drink?" Sasha asked. "No Pepsi or beer?"

"No. Just wine."

The Russians permitted Pepsi Cola to establish a bottling plant in the Soviet Union about ten years ago. Pepsi has sold well. It was expensive in 1974, when we visited, but now sells for forty cents a bottle, about the same price as in the U.S.

While we drank our wine and chatted, a Russian folk band arrived in their colorful silk blouses and peasant-style pants. They tuned their eight or nine balalaikas and an accordion and launched into some traditional Russian folk songs. I found my feet automatically tapping to the solid beat. I began clapping to keep time to the music.

"I don't think I can sit still much longer if they are going to play music like that," I told Gloria.

During the next slow number, the bandleader approached the tour director from a French tour group that was also dining in the restaurant.

"Won't you start the dancing?" he asked her. She declined.

"Let's dance?" I asked Gloria.

Several couples joined us after we had broken the ice. A few dances later, the band played a polka and we wore ourselves out whirling around the dance floor. The French group started off slowly, but about halfway through the evening, after the second or third bottle of champagne, things loosened up. A couple of attractive girls in their chic French fashions talked two middle-aged gentlemen into dancing a circle dance. They would break apart after dancing a short while and each get another partner. By ten o'clock, all fifty of the French tourists were out on the dance floor dancing one of the Russian stompers. They formed a snake line and wound through the tables of the restaurant, laughing and singing. Our meal was delightful, and the music topped off a perfect first night in the Soviet Union.

We reluctantly left the party around midnight, an hour after sunset in Leningrad at this time of year. With a restful night's sleep, we rose early to enjoy the first full day of our Soviet adventure. After a cafeteria-style breakfast of potato pancakes, cheese, liver sausage, boiled eggs, cereal, rolls, and tea, we went to Intourist to arrange a sightseeing excursion. We got tickets for an unaccompanied tour of the Hermitage (the former Winter Palace) in the morning and signed up for a guided tour of Petrodvorets (Peter the Great's summer residence) scheduled for after lunch.

The Hermitage was built by Catherine the Second during the mid-1700s. It covers two city blocks and contains 1,400 rooms. It has one of the finest collections of European art in the world, rivaling the Louvre, the Prado, and the British National Gallery. Gloria and I arrived just after the museum opened at 10:00 A.M. and went directly to the second floor. For the first half-hour, we were the only tourists in that section. We wandered through the galleries and marveled at the large number of Rembrandts, Reubens, Van Dykes, and Monets. There were huge chunks of blue-and-green malachite carved into giant birdbaths and elegant vases. The collection of mosaic pictures was breathtaking. Some were composed of colored stones no larger than a grain of sand, to form an intricate picture of a fairy palace awash with brilliant colors.

In each of the 1,400 rooms there is a little, gray-haired Russian lady attendant sitting in a chair watching so that patrons don't touch the paintings or sculptures.

"Her job must be one of the most boring in the world," said Gloria. "She sits from 10:00 A.M. to 5:00 P.M. with her hands folded across her lap, staring blankly at the wall, waiting for her tea break or lunch break."

It appears that these ladies have taken vows of silence.

"Maybe they have committed some crime against Russian society and this is a form of punishment," I told Gloria. "Maybe the crime wasn't serious enough to be sent to Siberia, only bad enough to guard the Hermitage. If they have behaved poorly, they are assigned to the fourth floor, the French Impressionists gallery. Hardly anyone ever goes up there. It would be like solitary confinement."

As we walked around the empty rooms, we noticed that 50 percent of the ladies were nodding, napping, or sleeping soundly. One lady almost fell out of her chair as we walked by.

In one room, I decided to take a photograph of a sparkling crystal chandelier resembling a fancy street lamp post, at least nine feet tall. I noticed the wiry little gray-haired attendant in her black dress and hand-knitted shawl squirming as I adjusted my shutter speed and focused the camera. She was muttering to herself and fidgeting around in her cane-bottomed chair. As I snapped my picture, she simply couldn't restrain herself any longer. She shot out of her chair with her tongue and finger going full speed.

"*Svet luchshiy zdes* [the light is better here]," she said, dragging me to her favorite spot.

"*Da. Pozhaluista*," I thanked her as I took another photograph, which showed off the lamp better. Once she started talking, she couldn't stop. In Russian she told us, "These doors come from a famous church; this china belonged to Czarina Catherine II; this vase was . . . "

As we left, she was still talking. I'm certain she was reprimanded for breaking her vow of silence.

In the afternoon, we took a bus tour of Petrodvorets, located on the shores of the Baltic a little to the southwest of Leningrad. This palace is famous for the beautiful gardens and fountains it contains. There are crystal-clear streams flanked by golden statues flowing down to the sea. Throughout the garden, Peter the Great had constructed a number of fountains in assorted designs and for various functions. There were lavish golden fountains, ornamental ones with chessboard designs, and a sundial. Then there were the fun fountains where the action took place. Peter would invite his guests to stop and rest at one of the picturesque spots to enjoy the colorful flowers, aromatic trees, or a cool breeze. If someone stepped on the right (or wrong) rock in the walkway, a series of sprinklers turned on, dousing anyone standing nearby or sitting on the bench. We stopped at a circular gazebo with a six-foot–diameter bench in the center.

"I think I'll try my luck," I said to Gloria and made a dash over the stone walk. I made it under the circular roof without getting drenched and was contemplating my dash out when one lady in the group stepped on a trigger stone.

"Ahhhhh . . . " shrieked half a dozen people standing near the gazebo. Water poured down from the edge of the circular roof with a gush. I was cozy and dry under the roof, but after a minute or so, I wondered if the water was ever going to shut off. From the inside, it looked like a heavy downpour. Finally it shut off, and I made a dash for drier territory.

"You should fix up one of those in the backyard at home," said Gloria. "Think of all the fun we could have with our friends and relatives."

For supper that evening, we chose a quiet meal in the hotel café. The clear broth with stuffed dumplings (piroshki) was scrumptious. That was topped off with sausage, cucumber salad, and black bread. We walked down to the Baltic after supper and watched the sunbeams skipping across the top of the waves as the sun skirted the horizon. You'd think catching a sunset would be a snap, but this far north at midsummer, it's nigh onto impossible. We finally gave up and went to bed so we'd be fresh for our drive to Novgorod.

Chapter 5
Novgorod: Ten Liters of Benzine

On Saturday we were up early, eager to launch off into the hinterlands. We left the hotel and toured the city once or twice, trying to find the main road to Moscow. Finally locating the right road, we were on our way to the ancient city of Novgorod, about 110 miles south of Leningrad, on the way to Moscow. I decided I couldn't avoid it much longer, so I'd better stop and figure out how you get gas, or benzine, here in the Soviet Union. I located a benzine station on the outskirts of Leningrad, pulled up to the pump marked "92" octane, got out, and went to the office. The lady in the office was protected by an impenetrable series of glass windows. She speaks to customers through a microphone and loudspeaker arrangement, and they communicate back through a small tray that she thrusts through her front window. I took out one of my ten-liter benzine coupons and deposited it in her outstretched tray. She drew my coupon into her domain, and I turned to walk back to the gas pump.

Soviet gas stations are strictly self-service. As I approached the car, the loudspeaker behind me blared, "*Chto eto takoe* [What is this?]"

I turned around and saw the lady attendant yelling at me. Still talking through the loudspeaker, she motioned for me to return to the window. I couldn't understand what the problem was. She gestured for me to come around to the side door and enter the office. There she handed me two fifty-liter gas coupons, repeating, "What is this?"

31

"Not mine," I said. I pointed to the ten-liter coupon on her desk, which I had placed in the box, and showed her the rest of my sequentially numbered coupons. She understood, but was now concerned because the coupon was for 98 octane gas, and I was at the 92 octane gas pump.

"Okay. I'll move to the other pump," I said.

I moved the car forward to the 98 octane pump and got out. I cleaned the cobwebs off the pump handle and started filling my gas tank. It was obvious that the 98 octane didn't get much use. The Russian cars run on 72 octane, and only foreign cars use the high octane. When the pump got to ten liters, it shut off automatically in response to the selector's setting, which the office attendant had made.

I looked around and realized the benzine station had no

Soviet gas stations are strictly self-service—no repairs, no toilets, no Cokes or candy, just gas.

service garage to fix flats or do minor repairs, no toilets, no Coke or candy machines, just benzine. I did notice a barrel of oil with a hand pump where you could fill your own container if you needed oil. As I drove off, I felt we had accomplished another hurdle in our Russian adventure.

Between Leningrad and Novgorod, the road passes through a small town or village about every ten miles. Most of the towns consist of twenty to forty wooden one-story houses. They have painted decorations and designs around the houses at window level. There were community wells about every fifth house, where people were filling water buckets to carry home. The rural houses had no running water or indoor plumbing. The main road went directly through the village. Houses were arranged one deep along each side, with no roads behind the houses, only fields. Even the larger villages and towns consisting of one or two hundred houses still stretched for a mile with houses one deep along each side of the road. About every twenty or thirty miles, there was a GAI station. The GAI (pronounced guy-ee and standing for Gosudarstvennaya Avtomobilnaya Inspektsiya) is the Russian version of the state police. They stand watch along the highway, check vehicle documents, and patrol the roads. It appeared that they stopped every fifteenth or twentieth vehicle for a check. Everyone, including Soviets, must have an internal passport to travel any distance. The GAI can tell from the first three letters on the Soviet license plates what district the car is from. If it's not local, he will ask for passports and for proof that you have reservations at your destination. Russians aren't allowed to casually drive into Moscow and take pot luck at a hotel. "Must be arranged in advance," we were advised by one of the other patrons in the benzine station.

Halfway to Novgorod, I spotted a blue-uniformed GAI officer standing in front of his station swinging his white-and-black–banded baton as we approached. I had the feeling he planned to have us stop for a document check. He simply

33

The typical rural Russian house is wooden or made of logs, with three or four windows in front and a door at the side. They usually have four rooms, with electricity and television but no running water.

strained to read our license plate as we drove past. In the rear-view mirror, I could see him run back to the station to call ahead to the next station. We had seen no other foreign cars during the hour-and-a-half drive from Leningrad, and by the amount of attention we got, I had the impression that foreign cars are a rarity on the road. It was comforting to know that the GAI was concerned about our well-being. I could have used some of that attention the previous day when I got lost on the way to Leningrad.

As we approached the next GAI station, I watched to see if the officer would greet us. Sure enough, he was standing by the road slapping his palm with his baton. I waved as we drove by, and he touched the bill of his cap. That was the last GAI station prior to Novgorod. Too bad. I was beginning to enjoy the attention.

As we approached Novgorod, we picked our way around the road construction that infected about half of the Soviet cities we visited. This 1,100-year-old city, with a population of about 150,000 people, had been heavily shelled during World War II, and except for its kremlin, most of the buildings are postwar.

I drove around the center of town and saw no signs or indication of the Intourist hotel. We stopped at the post office and asked the postmistress if she knew where the hotel was located. She gave me a blank stare, indicating that my limited Russian wasn't working. A man standing nearby was hammering a top on a wooden box he was about to mail.

"*Gostinitsa Intourist?*" he asked.

"*Da. Gde Gostinitsa Intourist* [Where is the Intourist hotel]?" He gave me directions in Russian: "Back up Main Street a ways, turn right a couple of blocks, and then left before the bridge." Fortunately, he had chosen words that I could understand.

We set out and followed his directions as closely as possible. Five minutes later, as I drove down a narrow street that was quickly running out of buildings, I began to question how well I had understood the Russian directions. Just as we were losing hope, we saw a three-story cement-block building marked "Intourist."

The Intourist agent in Leningrad had been right. It is not necessary for you to know. Just ask!

When Gloria and I checked into the hotel, the desk clerk asked, "Do you have a *mashina*?"

"Yes. It's parked out front," I explained.

"You must park it in the garage," she insisted. She called

the porter to unlock the garage and directed me around to the end of the building. The porter was already out there when I arrived, and he swung the big double doors open and motioned me inside. When I drove into the dark underground cavern, I noticed an ancient gentleman sitting in a semilit office inside the basement. The garage had the appearance of a dark wine cellar. I parked the car and got out, commenting on the dank, musty odor and wondering how long it had been since someone had parked a car in there. The gentleman motioned me over into his office as I started to leave the garage. He wanted to know my license number, the make of the car, and my home address. Since mine was the only car in there, it seemed absurd, but he insisted. Watching this ancient Russian laboriously print the information I had given him, I got the feeling I was dealing with the Russian equivalent of Ed, the guy who used to guard Jack Benny's vault. I half expected him to ask me how Roosevelt or Stalin was doing or how the war was going.

Through the desk clerk, Gloria and I arranged for an Intourist guide to give us a walking tour of the city. Our guide was Nadya, a woman in her early twenties who had just graduated from the local pedagogical institute (teachers' college), specializing in the English language. She was neatly dressed in brown corduroy Levi jeans and a beautiful hand-knit sweater. Nadya started our tour with a short history lesson.

"Novgorod is one of the oldest cities in Russia. It was settled during the ninth century by two Slavic tribes and a Finnish tribe. The early chronicles say that in 862, the people who lived in the vicinity of Novgorod asked their Viking neighbors to take them in hand and help order their affairs. 'Our land,' they are reputed as saying, 'is great and rich. But there is no order in it. Come and rule over us.'

"The Norsemen, it appears, responded readily to the invitation, and after a preliminary reconnaissance, Prince Rurik

The typical Soviet hotel room has twin beds, a desk, a chair, and a lamp. The bed usually is covered with a pillowcase-type sheet that houses the blanket to keep it clean.

of Jutland established himself in Novgorod and became founder of the first Russian ruling dynasty.

"For a few hundred years, Novgorod paid tribute to Kiev, the early capital of Russia. By the twelth century, Novgorod had established itself as an independent principality with a population larger than Paris and they stopped paying tribute to Kiev. A kind of democracy prevailed, where the power resided with the assembly of its citizens. They elected the prince who was to rule them and the archbishop who was their spritual leader. If either displeased his subjects, he would be shown the way out of Novgorod.

"By the thirteenth and fourteenth centuries, Novgorod

became a major trade center, especially in furs, with a population exceeding 400,000. It fought back invasions of Tatars, Germans, and Scandinavians, but in the fifteenth century fell to Moscow.

"Novgorod proved to be a proud and troublesome subject of the czar in Moscow. Ivan the Terrible visited Novgorod in the 1570s and invited the city's stubborn prelates and magnates to a lavish banquet. In the midst of the festivities, the czar gave a prearranged signal and his henchmen rushed into the banquet hall and murdered the guests. That and subsequent invasion by the Swedish in 1610 completed the downfall of Novgorod.

"After occupying Novgorod for seven years, the Swedish king returned what was left of Novgorod to the control of Moscow. The city became a center of learning, but never regained its political and economic importance. It was occupied by the Nazis in World War II and almost totally destroyed," Nadya concluded.

As we came to the center of town, Nadya took us through the kremlin, where she pointed out buildings spanning a history of more than a thousand years. In the center, there is a beautiful bell-shaped monument commemorating the one-thousandth anniversary of Russia. It was erected in 1862 when our country was about to celebrate its one-hundredth birthday.

In the kremlin, we noticed a number of brides in white wedding gowns. We asked if they were going to be married here.

"No," explained Nadya. "In the Soviet Union, couples are married at the marriage palace. After the ceremony, it is customary for the newlyweds to visit the kremlin and place flowers at the monument of the unknown soldier."

Few people in the Soviet Union own a car, since they cost two or three years' wages and must be paid for in cash. Wedding parties usually travel by taxi. The taxis are decorated with ribbons, a pair of wedding rings on top of the cab, or wedding bells. During the hour we visited, there were four wedding parties filing in and out of the kremlin. As we entered the kremlin fortification, Nadya pointed out Saint Sophi's Church with its picturesque onion-shaped dome.

"This church dates back eight hundred years," she said, "and contains forty or fifty beautiful icon paintings from the thirteenth and fifteenth centuries. On top of the golden cupola sits a white stone dove. Legend tells us that a live white dove was sitting on the church when Ivan the Terrible came to Novgorod in the sixteenth century and plundered the city. The dove was so horrified by the atrocities of Ivan the Terrible's soldiers that it turned to stone.

"Grandmother told me," continued Nadya, "that as a girl she was told that Novgorod would survive as long as the dove remained on top of the church. In 1941, the Nazis shelled the town as they approached. One shell struck the church and blew the top of the dome off. The dove tumbled to the ground. After the Nazi occupation, our town of 100,000 people was reduced to just forty houses. Isn't it strange how legends come to pass?" she asked.

As we walked back to our hotel with Nadya, Gloria asked, "Did you knit your sweater yourself?"

"Yes," replied Nadya. "My mother taught me to knit."

"Where can I get a Russian knitting pattern? I've looked in all the stores."

"They are very hard to get," confided Nadya. "Usually clerks in the stores don't put them out on display, but hide them and only sell them to their friends and special customers. If you really want something, there are ways to get it. My mother is an avid knitter, and she is able to get the yarn and patterns she wants," explained Nadya.

"If I would send you some English knitting patterns, would you be permitted to send me a Russian pattern in return?" Gloria asked.

"Of course," agreed Nadya. "It would be permitted."

Before we left, Gloria and Nadya exchanged addresses and promises to send each other knitting patterns.

Gloria and I had heard of an exciting Russian restaurant that was located in part of the kremlin. "Could you make reservations for us?" I asked the hotel clerk.

She telephoned and told us, "They are full for tonight. It is Saturday and a lot of people are going out."

Our second choice was the restaurant in the Intourist hotel. They had a modern six-piece band complete with electric guitars, amplifiers, and drums. They mixed some rock-and-roll songs in with the folk music. The restaurant was filled with people by 8:00 P.M. Local Russian couples came to eat and have a good time dancing, judging from the number of champagne corks that popped. The couples were dressed fashionably with bright-colored dresses and dark suits. The Russians seem to make an evening of dining out. They drink a little, dance, eat appetizers, dance, start the main course, dance, drink, dance, and eat some more, and this continues for most of the night. They stop part of the way through the main course for another dance or two and then resume eating where they left off. It often takes three or four hours for them to finish a meal. The dance floor is always crowded.

In Novgorod, Gloria and I stopped by one of the department stores to browse and check prices. We found that a black and white nineteen-inch TV sold for $275, about the same as an equivalent one in the U.S. They had AM/FM radios that sold for forty-five or fifty dollars, but I noticed they didn't display any of the short-wave sets that could receive foreign broadcasts. In the clothes department, they had a beautiful collection of ladies' slips selling from twelve to eighteen dollars. That's probably why most Russian women don't wear slips. Pantyhose was priced at nine dollars and up. This encourages knee socks and short hose. A dressy turtleneck pullover sold for forty dollars. Well-made Soviet clothes appeared to be expensive when compared with Western prices. When you consider that most Soviet workers earn only $200 a month, you wonder how they can afford to dress as well as they do.

When we came to the knitting counter, Gloria's eyes lit up. "Buy me some Russian knitting needles and yarn," she urged.

We patiently waited in a queue for about five minutes to get near the counter. When it was our turn, Gloria pointed to the knitting needles.

"I'll take two pairs of those knitting needles and two balls of that brown yarn," she told the clerk in Russian.

The salesclerk doesn't collect the selections at that time; she writes down the price on a scrap of wrapping paper and hands it to you.

"Twenty-four rubles for two balls of yarn!" Gloria commented as we checked the prices that the salesclerk had written down. "That's over ten dollars an ounce, and it's not even wool. I don't see how these people can afford to buy yarn for a sweater."

I looked around for a cashier's station and found the one at the center of the store had the shortest line. We queued up and, after a two-or three-minute wait, paid for our purchases. We then queued up in the line to the counter to present our receipt and pick up our purchases. Another five-minute wait and our turn came. By this time, the clerk has forgotten who you are or what you wanted so you have to start all over again.

"I'll take two pair of those knitting needles and two balls of that brown yarn," repeated Gloria.

The clerk gets your purchases and lays them on the back counter. Then she prices them, and if you're lucky, they still come out to the amount on your sales slip. If so, she'll take

41

your receipt and then wrap the items. If not, you get to start the whole process over again. It took about thirty minutes to buy the yarn. If you want something from another counter, the whole procedure must be started over. Shopping for half a dozen items can turn into an all-day outing.

In the bookstore, there was a slight variation on the procedure calculated to make purchasing a little more difficult, especially for foreigners. When you tell the saleslady what you want, she just points to the cashier and tells you the price—no little slip of paper or anything. I went to the cashier and told her, "*Sorok kopeks* [forty kopeks]" in my best Russian and held out two twenty-kopek coins. She simply looked at me. The people behind me got impatient at our staring match, so I went back to the saleslady and pleaded for a little slip of paper.

"*Nyet*," she said, pointing to the cashier.

I considered forgetting the whole thing, but rejected that idea and returned to the cashier. I watched a young man walk up and drop thirty-five kopeks into the dish by the cashier. Without a word being spoken, she rang up thirty-five kopeks and gave him the receipt. So I got back in line. When my turn came, I dropped forty-kopeks into the dish and didn't say a word. Sure enough, she rang it up. Perseverance had paid off again.

Gloria and I then stopped at a toy store. To my surprise, there was a supermarket-type checkout station. You went around, picked out what you wanted, took it to the cashier, and she checked you out just like the good old U.S.A. I don't think it will catch on because it takes the sport out of shopping.

As we walked around Novgorod, we passed a shoe store that had a big tabby cat snoozing in the warm sun of the front window.

"I'll bet this cat owns the shoe store," said Gloria as she stopped to scratch his ears. The tabby opened one eye to see who his new friend was and then continued his nap when he saw we weren't going to buy anything. "That cat rates a star," said Gloria as she took out her pocket calendar, which she used to record important events.

Gloria tried in vain to coax a cat out with, "Kitty—kitty—kitty." "They don't understand English," our guide explained. When she tried, "Kosh—kosh—kosh," the cat came running.

Chapter 6
Kalinin: "It Is Written You Will Stay Here"

On Sunday morning, I reclaimed our car so we could continue our journey. The desk clerk called the porter to unlock the garage. The porter located the key and took me around to the underground vault. As he opened the big oak doors, I could see my friend in his subterranean office shielding his eyes against the hostile daylight.

"*Dobry den* [Good day]," I called as I made my way into the garage.

"*Dobry den*," he replied. "You go now?"

"*Da*. I go to Kalinin."

"Ah, Kalinin," he said with a blank stare, as though Kalinin might be somewhere on the other side of the earth. "You come back again?" he asked.

"*Da*. I will come back someday," I promised.

I backed my car out of the converted wine cellar and looked back to see the old garage attendant waving to me as the porter closed and locked the door to the tomb. I had the feeling I might be the last human being he'd ever see.

The 250-mile drive from Novgorod to Kalinin took about six hours as we competed with the trucks, tractors, and horse carts for the right-of-way. The countryside was flat and marshy. This marshland had been a major factor in keeping the Mongol Tatar hordes out of Novgorod in the thirteenth and fourteenth centuries. They found easier pickings in other areas of Russia and didn't want to fight the mosquitoes and the Russians at the same time.

At the first GAI station we passed, I noticed the officer

44

standing on the other side of the street chatting with two pretty girls. He didn't even turn around as we drove by. At the next station, fifty miles down the road, the officer was reading the newspaper. I got the feeling the state police didn't really care where we were today. This makes one feel so unimportant. During the entire 250-mile drive I never did catch their eye.

About three o'clock in the afternoon, we approached the city of Kalinin, an industrial community of 400,000 people on the Volga River, 150 miles north of Moscow. Intourist had advised us before we left Novgorod that we would be staying at the Seliger Hotel, in the center of the city. For directions, they told us to stop at the Tver Motel on the outskirts of town. I believed I could find the hotel with little difficulty, but to humor Intourist, I decided to follow their directions to the letter. When I went into the lobby of the Tver Motel, there was no one at the Intourist desk. I went to the receptionist and asked for directions to the Seliger.

"You see Intourist," the receptionist said.

"Where?"

"Down the hall, on the left."

I proceeded down the hall. The second door on the left was marked "Service Bureau." When I attempted to open it, it was locked. I knocked and waited. No answer. I started back to the reception desk and then heard the door open and close. I hurried back to knock on the door again. A pretty blond lady in her stocking feet answered the door.

"Directions to the Seliger Hotel?" I asked.

"You follow highway to center of town, can't miss hotel," she assured me. Then she returned to her TV program, which I had interrupted.

A second lady in the room called to me as I started down the hall, "*Familiya* [Family name]?" she asked.

"Johnson."

She sifted through a stack of papers and found the one

she was looking for. "Ah," she said, "it is written that you will stay here tonight."

"But Intourist told us this morning we would be at the Selinger Hotel," I argued.

"It is written you will stay here," she proclaimed. Since the tone of her proclamation made it sound like a divine prophecy, I could hardly refuse.

After we checked into the motel, I rummaged through my trip log and found my history notes about Kalinin. In 1175, it was founded as Tver, a name that it retained until 1933. It was an important river town (on the Volga) that rivaled Moscow, to which it fell in 1486. Tver developed into an important trading and transportation center in the eighteenth century, with the development of the Vyshnevolotsk Canal System. The town was destroyed by fire at the end of the eighteenth century and rebuilt with wide avenues and squares. River trade declined after construction of the Moscow-Leningrad railroad, which marked the start of Kalinin's industrialization. It was occupied briefly by the Nazis during 1941 and severely damaged during the Second World War.

Armed with this capsule history, we drove downtown to see the city. Most of Kalinin's population were out for a Sunday stroll in the park along the Volga. The park had a live concert in progress and a permanent kiddy carnival, both of which were filled to standing room only. Lines of neatly dressed Russian children with bows in their hair or smart little caps on their heads stood goggle-eyed watching the merry-go-round, swings, and a small Ferris wheel. The equipment was ancient, but the kids weren't interested in looks, just results. The wooden horses on the merry-go-round looked like they had been through the war—an ear off here, a hoof missing there, a bobbed tail or scarred nose. The animals displayed several dozen coats of paint, but from the way the children rode them, they might have been carved of ivory and trimmed in gold. For five kopeks the children were transported to a fairyland for a full five minutes.

The Russian children love to play in the fountains at the park. This young lady had all the composure of a professional model.

Gloria and I each bought a vanilla ice cream cone (the only flavor usually sold) and strolled through the park hand in hand, watching the young people going through their courting rituals. Public display of affection, such as hand-holding or sitting close together, is not condoned in the Soviet Union. The couples walked and talked or sat and gossiped, but always with a respectable distance between them. How frustrating that must be when you are falling in love!

The grocery stores were open on Sunday, but the clothing and other retail stores are open only six days a week. We stopped in a grocery to compare some food prices and found they were reasonable. Eggs were $1.35 a dozen, sugar $.77 a pound, milk $.40 a quart, bread $.44 a loaf, and wine about $3.00 a bottle.

When we drove back to the motel on the edge of Kalinin, we found the large parking lot in front of the motel completely empty and pulled into one of the 150 parking spaces. As we got out of the car, I noticed a sign in front of the car: "NO PARKING FROM 7 TO 23 HOURS." I went inside and asked where we were supposed to park. The clerk motioned to the far end of the lot. I went back out and drove around the empty lot. At the corner of the lot there were five parking spaces marked: "TOLKO INOSTRANNYE MASHINY [FOREIGN CARS ONLY]." I parked there, figuring that later in the evening, a bunch of tour buses or something would come in and fill the lot. The next morning, our car was still the only one in the entire lot.

"Where shall we eat supper?" I asked Gloria.

"I don't know, but I'm starving for a pizza," she said.

"There's not a pizza within 600 miles of here," I told her. "How about a cutlet?"

"Do you think they have Chinese food?"

"The way they feel about the Chinese right now, we'd be more likely to find a McDonald's," I said. "Let's try the motel restaurant."

As we entered the dining room at 6:30, only two of the fifty tables were occupied. The waitress motioned us in the general direction of the windows. We chose one of the tables with a window view and got comfortable. The waitress came flying over and made it very clear that we were to sit at a table with two other people and fill that table. Okay. We moved. We introduced ourselves and sat down with a couple who looked to be in their forties. They spoke no English and no Russian. After sitting there for a few moments in total silence, I asked, "*Deutschland* [Germany]?"

"Nein. *Osterreich* [Austria]," the husband replied.

"Ah. We're from America."

We went on to exchange simple phrases and to pantomime when we got stuck for words. They were from Vienna and were taking a camper on a round trip of the Soviet Union and Europe, a trip very similar to ours. They had gone from Vienna to Czechoslovakia and Poland and into the Soviet Union. They had been in Moscow yesterday and planned to visit Novgorod and Leningrad next. Then they would proceed to Finland, Sweden, Denmark, Germany, and home. Except for Czechoslavakia and Poland, the trip was the same as ours, only in reverse order. Presently the husband excused himself and disappeared for a short while. He returned with a detailed map of Moscow and handed it to me.

"You need tomorrow," he said. "Moscow traffic very bad."

The waitress finally came to take our order.

"What'll you have?" I asked Gloria.

"You're sure they don't have pizza?" she asked as she scanned the five-page menu.

"Trust me."

"Two cutlets, one beer, and a Pepsi Cola," I told the waitress as Gloria went on mumbling about lasagna, canelloni, and spaghetti.

One of the advantages of moving into a new hotel each day is that you get a good sampling of the two hundred and fifty-six possible variations of being seated, ordering meals, and paying the bills. For breakfast, we went to the dining room at 7:30 A.M. We stood around in the empty room for a few minutes. A waitress finally came out of the kitchen and said, "Not open until 8:00."

We returned to our room and waited. At 8:00, we returned

to the dining room and still we were the only two people there. The waitress scurried around setting tables for the tour groups. She seated us and disappeared. Five minutes later, she brought out some black bread and placed it on the table along with some thin-sliced hard salami.

"You want omelets or fried eggs?" she asked.

"Omelets, please."

She disappeared again. Five minutes later, she returned and said, "No milk. You get fried eggs. Want coffee?"

"One coffee and one tea."

Another five minutes passed. She returned with our fried eggs, one coffee, and one tea.

Chapter 7
Moscow: "You Get Stroganoff"

We left Kalinin and pointed our Opel Kadett down Highway E-4 for Moscow. After three hours of dodging tractors, people, and cabbages, (bouncing off speeding trucks) we passed the motorway that circles Moscow. The landscape changed abruptly from rural to suburban and industrial. Our Austrian friend was right—Moscow traffic was a mess. I wanted to close my eyes as we headed for the center of town. It was written that we should stay at the Ukraina Hotel, a thirty-five–story fairy-book structure decorated like a wedding cake. About ten minutes into the city, I spotted a building that looked like the Ukraina and made my way across five lanes of traffic to the exit lane. As we pulled up to the hotel, I checked the map and the street sign.

"It's the wrong street," I told Gloria.

"That's because this is the Leningrad Hotel," she said.

It seems that the Russians liked this particular design so much they made seven similar buildings in Moscow based on the wedding-cake design. We took off again and, after passing two more wedding-cake buildings, finally found the Ukraina Hotel.

After going through the registration ritual, surrendering our passports, getting our tourist card endorsed, and finding the name of our hotel in the next city, we made our way to the elevator. The Ukraina Hotel was built thirty or forty years ago, but the elevator must have been old when it was first installed. It had a serial number of 001! I've seen slow elevators

51

before, but I watched as people put their luggage down by the elevator and then went to the coffee shop, ordered, drank their coffee, and got back long before the elevator got there. When we finally got on, it was a magnificent sight, with dark oiled mahogany paneling and gold tinted mirrors. The door shut; the elevator just sat resting up for the long climb. Once or twice the doors would open as though the elevator thought we might have decided to get out and walk up. But we persisted and stood our ground. After a few minutes, it grudgingly started up, with a lot of creaking and clanging. It made it to the mezzanine and decided to stop there and rest awhile. The doors opened slowly and the machine silently pleaded for us to get out. The little motors started up again, and the doors laboriously closed. On it went, up one floor at a time, wheezing, straining as it got to each floor. By the time we got to the eighth floor, I was exhausted. We put our luggage in our room and read the notice describing the four different restaurants in the hotel.

"Let's try Number Two," said Gloria.

"Only serves group tours," I said.

"How about Number Three?"

"Only open for the evening meal."

"Then let's go to Number One."

"That one closes at 1:30, five minutes from now."

"That only leaves Number Four."

"Good choice," I agreed. "Let's walk down. I'm too tired to ride the elevator."

Restaurant Number Four serves two different *komplekt* or meals-of-the-day. The contents of each *komplekt* were listed at the entrance.

"I can only make out about every other item on the list," I said to Gloria.

"Well that's soup and that's ice cream," she said, pointing to familiar words on the menu. "The rest is Greek to me, too."

52

We chose the meal with the soup and ice cream and hoped for the best. I paid the cashier and got two meal tickets. The maitre d' seated us at a table with a stern-looking Russian couple who were grumbling about the service or something. The waitress came by and asked us something in Russian.

"What did she say?" asked Gloria.

"Wants to know what we want to drink," I explained confidently. "One beer and one mineral water," I told the waitress in Russian.

"Sure is busy," said Gloria.

"Only restaurant open this late in the afternoon."

The waitress brought our soup and a few moments later, the rest of the komplekt. It was a dish heaped with cooked barley, meat with a gravy broth over it, black bread, and a dill pickle. The waitress had forgotten our drinks, so I flagged her down the next time she sailed by our table.

"One beer, one mineral water," I ordered.

"No ticket," she insisted.

"What ticket?" I asked.

"You pay for drinks at cashier when you order meal," she explained. "No ticket, no drink."

"Bring the ice cream then," I pleaded. I was full of barley and black bread and needed something to wash it down.

Since there was no TV in the room, I spent our first night in Moscow rereading the history synopsis in the Russian Intourist guide.

The birthday of Moscow is officially set as A.D. 1147, hundreds of years after Novgorod, Kiev, Suzdal and Vladimir were flourishing. The first wood kremlin was erected on the banks of the Moscow River by Prince Yuri Dolgoruky (The Prince of Suzdal) in 1156. By the 13th century it had become the center of the Moscow principality. In the later part of the 13th century Moscow was captured by the Mongol Tatars, but the rule of Batu Khan did not last long.

53

With Moscow back in Russian control in 1326, the foundations of first stone building, the Uspensky Cathedral, were laid. By 1328 Moscow superceded Vladimir as the chief seat of sovereignty. In 1380 the army of Prince Dimitri left from Moscow to defeat the Tatar forces at Kulikovo on the Don. During the last half of the 14th century the present Kremlin rose to become the residence of the ruling prince and a fortress to withstand the attacks of the Mongol Tatars, Lithuanians and others.

By the 15th century Moscow had established its permanent role over the various Russian principalities and its urban area was over three square miles.

A hundred years later it had grown into the capital of a strong and prosperous state, one of the largest in the world. In 1547 Ivan the Terrible became the first Russian Sovereign to be crowned Tsar. Russian prospered during his fifty years of harsh rule. In 1555 Ivan commissioned two Russian architects, Barma and Pustnik, to build the Cathedral of St. Basil the Blessed in Red Square. The unique structure which resulted combined nine churches with a central structure 107 feet high surrounded by eight tower-like chapels linked by elevated galleries. Each chapel had a unique cupola signifying that all the different Russian tribes were united under one God and one Tsar. It is said that Ivan had the architects blinded after St. Basil's was completed so it could not be duplicated or rivaled.

A series of tragic wars, fires and invasions plagued Moscow during the last half of the 16th century and first half of the 17th century. With the strong leadership of Peter the Great, toward the end of the 17th century Moscow entered a new era of stability and development.

Even when Peter moved Russia's capital to St. Petersburg in 1713, Moscow still remained the economic and cultural center of the country. The first university was opened in 1775. The city suffered a setback in 1812 when Napoleon entered the city and three of every four buildings were destroyed. But Moscow rose from the ruins and by 1840 was completely rebuilt.

In 1918 the capital was moved back to Moscow and its growth continued. In the early stages of World War II Moscow was hard pressed by the Nazis. The enemy was stopped during the bitter winter of 1941 almost under the walls of the city and for many months Moscow was repeatedly attacked from the air. The post-war period saw the end of the Stalin era and the realization of the second urban plan, which emphasized housing. Thousands of apartment buildings sprang up to replace the houses destroyed during the war and house the city's rapidly growing population.

On our first morning in Moscow, Gloria and I planned a sightseeing trip around the city. We decided to take the metro to the USSR Exhibit of Economic Achievements, located on the north side of the city. It consists of thirty to forty exhibits, each displayed in its own building. There are displayed the latest achievements in transportation, space, forestry, farming, culture, atomic energy, et cetera. It is like a permanent world's fair, only with more practicality-minded exhibits. Not only do they show off the latest products, but people are brought in from various parts of the Soviet Union for one- or two-week seminars on the newest technology. The fish-management workers from Siberia spend two weeks at the fishery exhibit learning the latest information available about fisheries. Others are concerned with mining, timber management, animal husbandry, or farming. People attending these seminars live in bungalows or apartments on the exhibition grounds.

I spent most of my time in the space exhibit, while Gloria visited the printing and book exhibit. There are a host of satellites on display in the space exhibit, including a full-size model of the world's first satellite, Sputnik, and the Apollo/Soyz space vehicles, mated as they did in space in 1975. There also was an exhibit of the Soviet moon lander, the dog, Laika, used in the early space experiments, and an automatic weather-satellite station.

The exhibit park was filled with dozens of fountains and

gardens. One fountain had fifteen beautiful golden statues of women depicting the fifteen republics that make up the Soviet Union. There were many children playing in the fountains while their parents sat on the benches chatting. I fell in love with a five-year-old blond girl wearing a red-and-black dress with shiny red shoes and a red hair bow. She sat on the edge of the fountain and posed with a million-dollar smile while I took her picture.

I planned to jog while I was in Moscow, but I was openly skeptical about how my early-morning run would be viewed by the bureaucratic establishment. I tried to sneak out of my room at dawn, but the key lady on our floor had a built-in security alarm that let her know when anyone was stirring. She was sitting at her key desk napping as I silently closed the door to my room and tiptoed toward the stairs.

When I passed the desk, she opened one eye and demanded, "Where are you going?"

"Exercise," I explained.

"Key," she demanded as if I planned to sell it on the black market.

Once outside, I headed down a grassy path along the Moscow River for what I expected to be a lonely run. You can imagine my surprise when I encountered my first Russian runner, a slightly built woman in her early twenties. In the next mile, I realized how wrong I'd been. I passed twenty or thirty individual runners, most of them in Adidas T-shirts and running shoes. There was almost a traffic jam of runners, dog-walkers, and fishermen along the river. There were even a few swimmers, one of whom was challenging a gravel barge for the right-of-way on the Moscow River. Running is "in" around Moscow these days.

A visit to Moscow would not be complete without a tour of the Kremlin (the Russian word for "fortification"), the symbol of the Soviet Union's power and perseverance. We joined a guided tour and hiked first to the Oruzheinaya Palace, or the Armory. The first hall contained a magnificent collection of armor, including a miniature suit of armor worn by Peter the Great when he was ten years old. The second and third halls contained jewelry made by Russian and foreign goldsmiths and silversmiths. There was a collection of royal clocks, including a gilded copper clock in the form of a book that had belonged to Ivan the Terrible and a wooden clock made by Russian workmen in the nineteenth century. There were the famous Fabergé Easter eggs. One silver egg had a map of the trans-Siberian railroad engraved on the outside and inside a golden clockwork model of a train with a platinum engine, crystal windows, a windup motor, and a tiny ruby for a headlight.

Another hall housed the royal thrones, the oldest of which was a veneered one with carved ivory that had belonged to Peter the Great. One of the thrones displayed there was presented to Czar Boris Godenov by the shah of Persia. It was carved with plates of gold and studded with 2,200 precious stones and pearls.

Next we visited the Cathedral of the Assumption, which was built in 1475. This church-museum is topped with five gold cupolas. It contains rare paintings, including an icon of the Virgin of Vladimir.

We toured three other nonworking churches—the Church of the Disposition of the Robe, the Annunciation Cathedral, and the Cathedral of the Archangel.

The tallest building in the Kremlin is the Bell Tower of Ivan the Great. This octagonal tower is 263 feet high. A second bell tower was built beside the main tower in the mid-1500s. Together they have twenty-one huge bells, the largest weighing 70 tons.

Nearby on the square stands the Csar's Bell, the largest bell in the world, weighing almost a half-million pounds (the weight of a Boeing 747 aircraft). It was built in the early 1700s, and a chunk was broken off before it was hung, so it has never been rung.

Not far from the bell stands the Czar's Cannon. This cannon, which was cast in 1586, weighs 80,000 pounds. It was designed to fire a cannonball thirty-six inches in diameter. The cannon was apparently built as a bluff, because it has never been fired.

We toured a few more museum buildings, and as we were leaving the Kremlin through one of the huge gates, our guide called our attention to the red star on top of the gate tower.

"Made from thousands of rubies. At night it gives off a red glow from the natural brilliance of the rubies."

We passed the Kremlin gate later that night, and I stopped to admire the brightness of the ruby star's glow. I'll bet a nickel to a hole in a doughnut there's an electric light bulb in the middle of that star.

Back at the hotel as we rested up from our Kremlin tour, Gloria asked, "What are we going to do for excitement this evening?"

"How about touring the metro?" I suggested.

"Are you crazy?"

"No. I mean it. I've seen pictures of some of the subway stations, and you won't believe how beautiful they are," I said.

"Is this one of your sick jokes?"

"No. I'm serious. If you're not impressed with the subway, I'll buy you one of the those sticky cakes with all the icing and strawberries on it that you keep drooling over."

"It's a deal. Sticky cake, here I come."

The metros were started in the 1930s and are constantly being expanded. They move over half the 8 million inhabitants of Moscow every day. For the low fare of five kopeks (seven cents) it is a twenty-minute ride to anywhere in Moscow. You enter the system by dropping a five-kopek coin in an automatic gate and rushing through before the metal arms reach out and grab you.*

The metros are the deepest subways I've ever seen, most running 300 feet below ground. You are whisked down by the fastest and longest escalators in the world. When you step onto the moving stairs and look down, you get the feeling you are falling into Alice's rabbit hole. As you hurtle down at express speeds, you catch a glimpse of the frenzy at the bottom of the stairs. Metro guards are whisking the people away from the bottom of the stairs to keep the area clear for the army of people behind them. If anyone should stop for even a second, there would be an enormous mountain of people stacked up in no time.

The metro system consists of seven lines radiating from the center of the city and a circular line connecting them, each identified by its own distinct color on the metro map. The trains run in each direction from a station on a tight timetable. During peak traffic hours, a train leaves every two minutes in each direction. There are two clocks on the platform; one tells real time and the other tells how long since the last train departed. As we stood and watched the rush-hour traffic, I saw three trains come and go. Each pulled into the station about one minute after the previous one left, discharged

---

*During our 1974 trip to Moscow, Bob, my cousin's husband, put his coin in and darted through the gate. The alarm bells went off, a red light flashed, and two metal arms shot out to seize the trespasser. A burly metro matron in her official blue uniform rushed over, shouting excitedly in Russian. Bob stood there bewildered, wondering what crime he'd committed. The metro matron rushed up and began beating Bob about the back and shoulder. As we rushed back to defend him, we found out that he had put his money in one gate and then gone through the wrong gate. The metro matron was not the least bit concerned about the alarm. She had noticed that Bob had brushed up against the whitewash on the side of the metro tunnel and had the white dust all over the shoulder of his coat. She finished brushing him off to her satisfaction and let us proceed on our way as she went to shut off the alarm and flashing light.

its passengers, loaded again, and was off before the clock reached "two minutes." Watching this drama, I noticed that most of the train conductors were women. As I pointed this out to Gloria, the attractive lady driving the metro smiled at us, waved, gunned her train, and sped away from the platform.

There are about eighty-nine metro stations in Moscow, of which a dozen are unusual enough to be cited in the tour guide. Each station has a different mode of decoration and motif. The Ploshchad Revolutsii Station near the Bolshoi Theater has beautifully carved ceiling supports, crystal chandeliers, and thirty or forty bronze statues depicting various aspects of rural life. The Komsomolskaya Station across from Hotel Peking has dozens of brilliant mosaics showing famous battles of Russian history. The Novoslobodskaya Station, a few blocks from the Central Theater of the Soviet Army, has a series of four-by-eight–foot stained-glass windows between each of its sixty-four pillars. Each is unique and backlighted, which makes the station look like the inside of a church.

"I can't believe how immaculate the stations are," said Gloria. "There's no litter on the floor or graffiti on the walls. They are like museums or theater lobbies."

As we boarded our fourteenth metro and headed back to the Ukraina Hotel, I asked Gloria, "Was it worthwhile?"

"Yes, but don't you think we could stop for a sticky cake anyhow?"

Another must in Moscow is a tour of the big department store GUM. It is located on Red Square, directly across from the Kremlin. Years ago, Red Square was a marketplace. Then the Russians decided to get neat and built the government department store, moving the market indoors. The market still consists of several hundred individual shops, each located in its own particular niche. Here, in one spot, it is possible to find the various goods sold throughout the city.

We stopped by the knitting shop and found they sold the same items that we had bought in Novgorod and for exactly the same price. Their selection appeared to be a little greater, but due to the haphazard display of the merchandise, it was difficult to tell. In one of the souvenir shops, we found a collection of Russian enameled pins and boxes. The saleslady told us of the small town near Vladimir that had turned out icons for the churches. After the revolution, the artist turned to enamel painting on a black background to make a living.

The GUM department store contains several hundred shops, with a variety of merchandise, from shoes to jewelry to food.

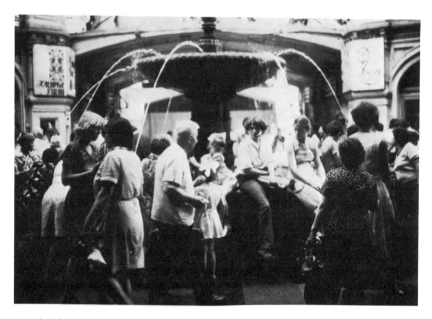

The fountain in GUM is a favorite meeting place for shoppers.

"I must have that pin," said Gloria, "the one with the woman spinning yarn by hand."

"How about this winter scene?" I asked, pointing to a box with a fellow driving a sleigh pulled by three magnificent horses.

"That's a fantasy scene," said Gloria as she identified the weird creatures lurking in the swirls and decorations in the background.

We bought the pin and a book telling how the items were made. As we made our way around the main store, we came upon a giant indoor fountain extending up to the second-floor balcony. There were dozens of children from two to fifteen years old sitting around the fountain waiting patiently for their parents to return and claim them.

"Notice how well dressed and well behaved they are,"

said Gloria. "If this was the U.S., they'd probably be swimming in the fountain or filling it with detergent."

The store was packed with shoppers elbowing their way throught the aisles. Since it was a warm June day, we decided to try some of the famous Russian *morozhenoe* (ice cream). Everyone else in the store had a cone in their hand. We looked to see which direction people with the largest cones were coming from. I discovered they came from all directions. Finally, we located a central ice-cream–dispensing room with thirty or forty ladies hand dipping the rich vanilla- or chocolate-flavored ice cream and placing it on trays. Runners then took these trays out to the portable stands scattered throughout the store. The stand lady takes your twenty kopeks and you select an ice-cream cone from the tray. Every stand I went to had a line of twenty or thirty people. The trays held only sixteen cones. After watching three or four stands sell out before I could get to the head of the line, I decided to try to catch one of the ice-cream runners. It didn't work; they always traveled in pairs. I finally stood at a stand until the new supply came and got cones for Gloria and me. They were worth the wait.

For supper Gloria and I went to the Rossiya Hotel and ate in a dining room called The Attic. After surveying the menu, we each decided to order a number of items from the a la cart menu. The waitress dutifully wrote down each item we ordered. About fifteen minutes later, she came back with our food and proceeded to announce as she walked around the tables placing dishes in front of us, "You get Stroganoff and Stroganoff for you." If you eat late in the evening, you get whatever is left in the kitchen.*

*We had quite a different experience in Leningrad. Again, Gloria and I both ordered different items—salad, soup, main course, dessert. The waiter stood by the table nodding as we ordered. He did not write down a single item. Much to our surprise, when he returned with our food, not only did we get exactly what we had ordered, but he remembered who ordered what. That was one of the few professional waiters we met in the Soviet Union.

While in Moscow, I called a Russian acquaintance of a friend of mine. She works on the foreign-language staff at the Moscow Automobile and Road Building Institute. The institute teaches civil engineering related to roads, bridges, airports, and tunnels. After three or four interesting wrong numbers, I finally got through to the institute.

"*Slushayu* [I'm listening]," the switchboard operator answered.

"*Juli Sergeva, pozhaluista*," I requested.

"*Vy ozhldaite* [You wait]."

"*Slushayu*," answered Juli after a short wait.

"This is Allen Johnson, a friend of Ed Rupp," I said.

"Ah, yes, Mr. Johnson. Ed wrote me about you."

"My wife and I would like to come out to your institute and meet you, if that would be possible."

"Yes, I'd love to meet you. Would tomorrow morning be convenient?"

"Yes. Would nine o'clock be okay?" I asked.

"Fine," Juli said. "Come to 64 Leningrad Avenue, and I'll meet you at the reception desk."

As we drove out to Leningrad Avenue the next morning, I had Gloria watch for building numbers while I kept an eye on traffic.

"There's Number 44," yelled Gloria after we passed the train station. "It's probably in the next block."

Ten blocks later, we were only up to 56. The Russians are very stingy with their house numbers. One number will often do for an entire block of buildings. A few more blocks and Gloria spotted 64. I pulled in behind the building and parked in the faculty parking lot.

The institute was a gray stone building filling the entire block. The entrance was in the center of the block and was equipped with a dozen stone benches, an oval flower garden, and a flagpole.

We walked into the spacious reception hall and immediately caught sight of a middle-aged lady dressed in a blue flowered dress with an "I love NY" button on her lapel.

"Ms. Sergeva?"

"Yes. Mr. and Mrs. Johnson, I presume?" she answered in perfect English with a trace of a Russian accent. "I wore my New York button so you'd be sure to recognize me."

"There don't seem to be many students here this morning," I said.

"It's examination time now, and they only come in on the days of their examinations," Juli explained.

We walked down a series of gray halls and up several flights of worn stone steps to Juli's office on the third floor. She showed us a typical classroom on the way. It was similar to the room in which I studied English composition at the University of Illinois, with rows of desks and straight-backed chairs, a long table on a slightly raised platform for the instructor, and a blackboard covering one wall.

"After secondary school, a student may compete for entrance into the various technical institutes, pedagogical institutes, or vocational schools," explained Juli. "Our students in the Automobile and Road Building Institute are nearly equally divided between male and female. All students must take a foreign language. It's to help them read the technical journals, which are in English, German, and French."

"Is there any research conducted at your institute?"

"Oh, yes. Our facility conducts original research in civil engineering. We don't have research laboratories in our industrial companies, so the institutes are charged with doing the theoretical and applied research."

Juli took us around the institute to see the extensive computer facilities, laboratories, libraries, and lecture halls. After the tour, she brought us back to her office for tea.

"What do you do for relaxation?" Gloria asked.

65

"During the summer, I walk in the woods or sit in the park and read. In the winter, I ski a little and visit old friends," replied Juli.

"Oh, can you ski to work in the winter?" Gloria asked.

"No," said Juli. "I live in the country about twenty miles from here. I ski in the woods."

We drank our hot, sweet, strong Russian tea and chatted for half an hour.

"Would you be kind enough to do me a favor?" asked Juli.

"Sure, if we can," said Gloria.

"I have some gifts that I would like to send to Ed Rupp and his children, but I'm afraid they will not survive the mail. Would you take them back with you and give them to him?"

"Of course," we agreed. She gave us a bag filled with *matryoshka* (dolls nested inside of dolls), miniature pottery, a picture book of the Kremlin, and a large book with pictures of rural Russian scenes and historical buildings.

"And for you," Juli said as she handed Gloria another bag filled with *matryoshka*, a small decorative teacup, and a book about Leningrad.

Luckily, Gloria and I had brought some gifts my cousin Pat had hand-knitted. We gave Juli a knitted belt in return.

"I hope you will visit me again when you return to Moscow," Juli commented as she walked us to our car.

"We'd love to come in the winter and ski with you," Gloria said as we shook hands and drove back to the hotel.

That evening, we planned a trip to the circus. I don't believe any people enjoy the circus more than the Soviets. Maybe it's because they are still a rural people at heart and because it is one of the greatest forms of humor in the Soviet Union. Every city of any size in the Soviet Union has its own permanent circus. We visited the new circus on ice in Moscow. As is customary, we got front-row seats because we were foreigners. This new circus was performed entirely on ice. All the acrobats, jugglers, and clowns wore ice skates. The technical details of lighting, sound, and props are handled with the precision of the Rockettes of Radio City Music Hall. The music is provided by an orchestra, complete with piano, violins, oboe, and a harp. The most unusual act was a half-dozen Russian brown bears playing hockey. They had a goalie and two forwards on each team. They had real hockey sticks and a standard puck. The human referee would drop the puck, and the bears would bat it toward the goal. The goalie nearest our side of the arena would turn the goal over if the puck got too close.

The most unusual act at Moscow's new circus on ice was the Russian brown bears. They played hockey like pros, with the goalies resorting to some clever moves to prevent scoring.

The referee would skate up and chunk the bear on the noggin with a hockey stick to get his attention and warn him not to turn his goal over again. Play would resume and as the puck came down to our end, over went the goal again. The bear would turn to the audience as though he were seeking approval for his action. The crowd roared and clapped; the bear would bow in acknowledgment. They never made a single goal on him. I was astounded at how well the bears skated. Then I noticed they were wearing double-runner skates. That was quite an act!

The audience thrilled to the agility of a balancing act where a performer did a headstand on top of a twenty-foot pole, balanced on the second man's head while he was skating slowly around the rink.

The stars of the circus are the clowns. Oh, how the Soviets love to laugh! The clowns act out the latest bureaucratic jokes, wondering, for example, how they could supply their space lab with all the necessities of life but a Muscovite couldn't find a safety-razor blade in the city. The crowd roared at the clowns running around with briefcases, stopping to fill out stacks of forms for every little thing they did. The circus is definitely the Russians' main outlet for humor, and it plays to a sellout crowd every night.*

At breakfast, I realized how formal and unbending Moscow is compared with other Soviet cities that we had visited. Breakfast was served buffet style. There was no coffee, only iced tea. We asked the waiter if we could get coffee.

*On our previous trip, we had watched as the clown portrayed a tipsy drunk on his way home. As he got around in front of my cousin Bob's seat, he sat down on his briefcase at the edge of the rink to rest. He sat there teetering back and forth, about to fall into the audience. After leaning at an exaggerated angle half a dozen times, he did fall out of the rink. Bob and another man sitting next to him jumped up to help him climb back into the raised rink. Once the clown got righted, he extended his hand to Bob to shake hands. Bob reached up to shake his hand and backed up to sit down. The seat had sprung up when Bob got up, so he missed the seat and sat on the floor. The clown was delighted. The whole audience joined in the laughter as Bob dusted himself off and sat down again.

"*Nyet*," he said. "Coffee in the coffee bar."

Elsewhere we were able to get coffee for breakfast. In a few places it was even possible to get milk to put in it, but not in Moscow. After breakfast, I went to the reception desk, where I had left our passports, and asked to get them back before we left.

"*Nyet*. You go to passport office on the second floor at 9:00 A.M.," was the reply.

At 9:00, I wandered around the second floor until I found a door marked "Passports." I went in and asked for my passport.

"Name?"

"Johnson."

"Nationality?"

"U.S.A."

The lady found my passport and filled out a receipt, which I had to sign. Elsewhere I had gotten my passport back from the reception desk where I had left it and seldom had to sign anything. Moscow is Moscow!

"Shall we walk up or take the elevator?" I asked Gloria after breakfast.

"Let's walk. We don't have time to wait for the elevator."

When we got to the eighth floor, we were challenged by the key lady.

"Room card," she demanded. She'd seen us coming and going fifteen or twenty times in the past two days, but we still didn't get through without the password.

"Eight-seventeen," I said, showing her our authorized room card. In a few cities, we had actually been allowed to carry our keys off the floor down to the lobby, but not in Moscow. The key ladies run their floor like a captain does his ship, and they run a tight ship. Nothing goes on without their knowing about it.

Even access to the lobby of most hotels in the Soviet Union is tightly controlled. The stated purpose of this control is to protect the tourist. The doorman, or guard, checks your key card when you enter the hotel to make certain that you belong. This security was evident from Moscow to Odessa and Yalta.*

After packing, I dropped off the key with the key lady and started for the elevator.

"Wait! You must have exit slip. How many bags do you have?"

"We have five bags."

She checked with the front office to see if I had paid my bill and then wrote out an official-looking document with my birthday, color of my eyes, passport number, room number, and number of bags and signed it.

"You must present this to the doorman in order to leave the hotel," she said.

The doorman looked like a wrestler or weight lifter. He checked the documents and then opened the door for us. In other cities, you simply dropped the key at the desk and left, but not in Moscow.

Once outside, I first checked my car to see that all the parts were there. The lady at the reception desk had warned us not to leave anything of value in the car. (That's probably pretty good advice for any large city anywhere in the world today.) A quick inventory showed that I still had four tires, a battery, a mirror, and the gas cap. Nothing appeared to be missing. We said farewell to the Ukraina Hotel and headed east.

---

*On our previous visit to the Soviet Union, we had stayed at a traditional old hotel in Yalta called the Oreander, located on the shore of the Black Sea. One evening after supper, we decided to walk along the shore and absorb the beauty of the full moon shining across this inland sea. We got taken in by the romantic beauty of the monent and did not get back to the hotel until 10:30 or 10:45 P.M. The place was locked up tight. We had to beat on the huge oak door to get the porter to let us in. The key lady waited at the top of the stairs, tapping her foot impatiently. She gave us a stern lecture about being late. We had to promise not to go out after 10:00 P.M. again without letting her know in advance.

Chapter 8
Yaroslavl:
"May I See Your Travel Documents?"

Gloria and I crossed the Moscow River and headed for Yaroslavl, about 150 miles northeast of Moscow on the Volga River. We were making good time on our way out of town until we got to the circular motorway around the city. A traffic policeman standing in the middle of the road signaled for us to pull over to the center divider. He came over and politely asked in Russian, "May I see your travel documents?" I produced passports, visas, and our tourist card. He scanned the list of sixteen cities that we were authorized to visit and smiled.

"Have a safe trip," he said in Russian as he handed the documents to me. This was our first actual encounter with the GAI. He had given us no cause for anxiety.

The road from Moscow to Yaroslavl began as a divided motorway for the first fifty miles. It isn't quite an expressway, because there are bus stops, pedestrian crossing zones, and a number of dirt or blacktop side roads that access at right angles. But there were no stops or villages along it. The countryside consists of rolling hills with lots of forests and meadows, some filled with young wheat. You get a panoramic view of the country as you cross the low hills and are able to see fifteen or twenty miles in all directions.

After the first fifty miles, the road reverted to the typical two lanes, with an infinite number of trucks going at 20 mph. You get a lot of experience passing other vehicles here. With a village about every five or ten miles, you are lucky if you can average 35 mph.

The tourist literature suggests bringing a spare wind-screen (windshield) if you plan to drive through the Soviet Union in a foreign car. I couldn't understand the reason for the suggestion until I drove behind a Soviet truck. The majority of the Soviet trucks are what we call state trucks or dump trucks. They have a six-by-eight–foot bed with two high sides. These trucks carried large rocks, gravel, timber, cement slabs, sugar, cabbages, bricks, or potatoes. The common practice is to heap the load on at least a foot higher than the side walls. When you get stuck behind a truck, it's not the oncoming traffic you have to fear; it's the foreign missiles bouncing off the truck. We often had to dodge cabbages, bricks, and two-by-fours, which flew off at every bump and turn in the road. There was not much chance of falling asleep from boredom.

As we approached the outskirts of Yaroslavl, which boasts a population of over half a million people, we passed several refineries and chemical plants. The city gets oil over a pipeline from the southern republics, and they ship the finished products out by way of Volga River barges.

Yaroslavl is an old city dating back to the ninth or tenth century, when Russia was first united. Prince Yaroslav, one of the four sons of the Prince Vladimir, who brought Christianity to Russia, settled in this area because of the good transportation offered by the junction of the Volga and Kotorosl rivers. The original fortification (kremlin) was constructed about 1010, and the city began to grow. The river offered a good trade route to Persia, India, and China, so the merchants built homes and storehouses in the city. In the sixteenth and seventeenth centuries, it was the third largest trade center in Russia.

It was the tradition of that time for the wealthy merchants to build their own churches. By the seventeenth century, there were eighty private churches in Yaroslavl, all with their picturesque, onion-shaped domes. Only fifteen of these seventeenth-century churches survive today. They add a beautiful and softening touch to the modern architecture that now surrounds them. A number of the churches still contain the priceless icons and frescoes from the sixteenth and seventeenth centuries. It is interesting that the large churches have no heat and were used only in the summer. A small, separate church was built nearby and heated for the six or seven cold months of the year.

These magnificent churches had a small congregation of thirty or forty people, consisting of the merchant's family and some invited close friends. The churches served primarily as a status symbol, indicating wealth and power. One practical note: the area beneath the church was used as a storeroom for the merchant's goods. The walls were six feet thick, and besides, who would rob a church?

Across from our hotel, the Yaroslavl, I spotted a café. Now a café in the Soviet Union is not the same as a café in Dayton, but it was worth a try. Gloria and I decided to stop for a snack. The café had a counter like that of a bakery, with sticky, sweet goodies in the glass showcase. There were meals like liver and onions or cutlet displayed behind the counter. The eating area was a dozen small, round, stand-up–style tables or counters, but no chairs.

"I'll take one of those gooey ones over there and the one that looks like an apple tart," said Gloria.

"Pick one or the other," I said.

"Okay. The gooey one and coffee."

I stood back and watched to see how the system worked in the café. It appeared that you decided what you wanted at the counter, then went back to the cashier on the other side of the shop and told her. She rang it up and gave you the receipt. There were no names on the various cakes, so I resorted to the word we had been taught for dessert—*sladkoe*.

"*Dva sladkikh, odin cafe, odin chai* [Two sweets, one coffee, one tea]," I told the cashier. She stared blankly at me.

"*Sladkoe*," I said.

She shook her head slowly. Then her face brightened with understanding. "Ah, *pirozhnoe* [cake]," she said.

"*Da, dva i cafe, i chai*," I repeated as I handed her one ruble.

"*Vosem desyat kopees*." She smiled and handed me the receipt and my change.

Once up to the counter it was easy. I pointed to what we wanted. There's no language barrier to pointing. Gloria and I ate our cakes and watched the Russians about us devour their snacks. After the snack, we were ready to tour the city, so we hired an Intourist guide, Irina, for a two-hour walking tour of Yaroslavl.

Before we left the Intourist office, Irina offered us some Russian tea and a short history of her town:

"Tradition has it that Yaroslavl was founded in 1010 by Prince Yaroslav the Wise. It is the oldest Russian city on the Volga. A kremlin was constructed, and the city grew as an outpost guarding the point where the Volga and Kotorosl rivers meet. In the early thirteenth century, it became the capital of the principality and rivaled Moscow. In the fifteenth century, it fell under the control of Moscow. Yaroslavl was repeatedly overrun by the Tatar Mongol hordes between the thirteenth and sixteenth centuries.

"In the sixteenth and seventeenth centuries, it developed into a major trading center on the trade routes from the White Sea down the Volga to the Caspian Sea and the Near East. The rise of Saint Petersburg in the eighteenth century marked the decline of trade for Yaroslavl and the growth of its industries. These industries currently include automobile factories, shipyards, cotton mills, and electrical-appliance works," she concluded.

On our tour, Irina showed us the cathedral with its one-hundred–foot–high bell tower. We climbed the bell tower, and from the top we were treated to a beautiful view of the medieval town of Yaroslavl. The old churches stretched above the trees, with their deep-red bricks contrasting with the green-tile onion-shaped roofs. The Volga River flowed off in the distance, with the golden sun shimmering on its smooth surface. The Volga beaches were covered with beach umbrellas and hundreds of bathers braving the sixty-five or seventy-degree weather to absorb the early-summer sun.

Gloria and I ate supper at the Yaroslavl Hotel restaurant. The hostess seated us and then explained the Russian menu. She recommended the soup and the main course and then made certain that we had ice-cold beer and mineral water to drink. Such luxuries were never provided in Moscow.

"I'll take a tomato salad after the soup," I said.

The Russian children were well dressed and full of the same curiosity you find in children of any country.

From the bell tower you could see the green-domed private churches of the wealthy sixteenth-century Yaroslavl merchants.

"I'm sorry, but we have no tomatoes. Will you have a cucumber salad instead?" she asked.

"Okay, cucumber." I sighed with a note of disappointment.

A few minutes later, our hostess returned. "If you can wait a short while, I'll send someone out to get tomatoes for your salad."

"Of course we can wait," I said with a smile.

We got our soup and about ten minutes later the waiter returned with a bowl of plump, red, ripe tomatoes, hard-boiled eggs, and scallions. He set it in the middle of our table. The young waiter did an excellent job of providing fast, courteous service, always serving from the right and removing items from the left.

Dinner consisted of our salad, clear chicken soup with noodles, beefsteak, mashed potatoes, sliced stewed apples, black and white bread, ice-cold beer, mineral water, and a big pot of coffee. The bill came to ten dollars for the two of us, including service charge. The service and atmosphere were first class. All that was lacking was an orchestra. If we had stayed a little longer, I have no doubt that would have been arranged.

After Yaroslavl, we drove back through Moscow and on to the medieval town of Suzdal. As we passed through Moscow, I realized how hot and oppressive a big city can be on a bright, sunny June day. I was looking forward to a drive in the country; it was 150 miles to Suzdal. About ten miles outside of Moscow, we came upon the GAI station.

The young officer saw us coming and signaled with his baton for us to stop. We pulled off the road, and I got out my documents. He greeted us in Russian and asked for the passports. In addition to the passports, he was interested in our tourist card, which is signed by the hotel Intourist agent each night to vouch that we stayed where we were supposed to. He went inside the station to make a phone call. About three or four minutes later, he came out, smiled, and returned our documents. He wished us a happy journey.

"*Do Svidaniya,*" I said.

"Good-bye," he called to me in English as I got back into the car.

About two hours out of Moscow, I noticed some thunderclouds building up. For the next few miles, I looked for a convenient place to stop and put on the windshield wipers, which had been under the front seat ever since we had entered the Soviet Union, a week ago. By the time I found a place to stop, the rain was coming down in buckets. It was sort of like a Charlie Chaplin movie. The highway was deserted, with all the cars and trucks parked by the side of the road. All the drivers, including me, were dancing around in the rain, running from one side of the car to the other trying to get the wipers positioned. I finally got them on, getting a shower in the process.

By late in the afternoon, we had covered the short drive from Moscow to Suzdal. The city was founded nearly 900 years ago and today has a population of about 10,000 persons. We followed the signs to the Intourist hotel, but managed to circle the city three times. Our hotel was a huge tourist complex on the edge of town. There were signs pointing out the direction to the complex as we entered town, but no signs as we drove by the hotel. There was not so much as a name on the hotel building. We finally decided that the group of buildings set back from the road must be the place and drove in.

Chapter 9
Suzdal: Lemons with Sugar

The tourist complex contained a 400-room hotel, a 100-room motel, several restaurants, three bars, a movie theater, and a beach for swimming along the river. We checked in and went to the restaurant for supper, where the hostess seated us with a young German couple. Using our limited German and Russian and their limited English and Russian, we found out they were driving from Berlin to Leningrad and back. They were camping most of the time, with an occasional stay in a hotel.

"Soviet camping facilities not good," said the young man. "Campsites are small, muddy, and no facilities. German campsites are much better."

"No place to wash up," said his beautiful wife. "Hotels can be expensive."

The supper menu was in Russian with no translations. We were in the process of translating the menu when the waitress approached our table. The German couple ordered two beers, and the waitress turned to me.

"Order me a beer," said Gloria.

"One *pivo* and one mineral water," I said.

The waitress grabbed the menus and left.

"I don't think we're going to get a chance to order anything else," I said.

In a few minutes, the waitress returned with our drinks.

"*Menyu, pozhaluista?*" I asked.

"*Nyet.* You had the menu," she said curtly.

79

"Please. I would like to order something to eat," I pleaded.

"You order one time, food, drink, all one time," she said.

"If you give us one more chance, we'll order everything," I promised.

"Supposed to order all one time," she repeated as she reluctantly gave us a second chance.

"Peasant's salad, beef Stroganoff, bread, and coffee for two," I said. We were stumped for dessert. From what we could understand, the choice was between prunes with fermented milk and lemons with sugar.

"We'll try the lemons with sugar," I told the waitress. She took the menus and stomped off.

The peasant's salad turned out to be fresh carrots, cabbage, and beets chopped up with some dried chopped meat sprinkled over the top.

"Delicious," said Gloria as we ate our salad and black bread. "Wonder what the lemons with sugar will be like?"

"Maybe it's lemon pudding or a lemon chiffon pie," I suggested.

When dessert came, it was exactly as stated—one sliced lemon with crystalized sugar sprinkled around it. It was served in a crystal compote, but there were no utensils. Trying to appear worldly and continental, we reached into the compote, took a lemon slice with our fingers, rolled it around in the sugar, and ate it. I'm sure the German couple spent the evening in the bar laughing about lemons with sugar. We certainly did.

I spent the remainder of the evening looking over the tourist brochures and catching up on local history. It is said that no town in the Soviet Union can boast of the architectural riches of Suzdal and none is more deserving of the name "museum town." The monasteries, churches, kremlin, and houses present an almost complete picture of Russian architecture, covering the 700-year span from the twelfth to nineteenth centuries. Suzdal was founded in 1028 on the banks of the

Kamenka River. It grew in influence and importance and by the end of the eleventh century was the capital of an independent principality. With the decline of the influence of Kiev, Suzdal was the religious center of Russia from 1113 to 1238. The city continued to grow in importance even after the capital of the principality was moved to Vladimir in 1157. The city was overrun and destroyed by the Tatars in 1238, which marked the beginning of its decline. The dominating Spaso-Yevfimiev Monastery was founded in the fourteenth century on the north edge of the city, surrounded by a high fortified wall and twenty massive towers. The towers date from the troubled sixteenth and seventeenth centuries, when strong fortifications were necessary and theological arguments were rammed home with the help of siege artillery.

During most of the thirteenth, fourteenth, and fifteenth centuries, Suzdal was under the Tatar yoke. The city was burned down several times, but eventually, a truce, agreeing to yearly payments of tribute to the Mongol Tatar leader Batu Khan, was worked out. In about 1500, the Tatar influence in the area was broken.

We got up at 6:00 A.M. on Friday and jogged from our hotel to Suzdal. As we passed a large field, I heard a loud truck approaching from behind us. Turning around, I found myself staring into the propellers of a biplane flying down the edge of the field about ten or fifteen feet above us. Gloria and I ducked as he made a wide, sweeping turn. The plane, which was apparently crop dusting, made a half-dozen more passes over the field and then flew away.

A black-and-white mongrel pup darted out of his yard and started following us at the next turn in the road. He thought jogging was a great idea and followed us for a mile or so until he got bored and trotted back toward his house. At the next turn, a little black sheep bounded out of the yard and scampered along in the field beside us. After a hundred yards or so, he tired of the game and turned around to go eat

grass with a huge cow that was tied to a stake in the front
yard of the nearby house.

As we continued, we met several people taking their cows
to pasture. They walk the cows down the middle of the road
to the field by the river, where someone sits with them all
day. Since there are no fences, the cow tender has to keep
watch for the day. When we took a walk in the evening, we
met about ten or fifteen cows coming back from pasture with
the cow tender walking behind. As each cow came to its house,
it would turn into the open gate and walk to the side yard.
The lady of the house would be waiting with pail and stool.
The cow would stop at the appointed place, and the Russian
lady would then sit down and start milking the cow.

*Most of the rural families have a milk cow. Because of the lack
of refrigeration and delays in transportation, it's difficult to get fresh
milk except in the small villages.*

After our run, we drove the car down to the Kamenka River and washed it, using the Soviet bucket I had bought in a Suzdal hardware store the day before. It had rained cats and dogs, and the car was a mess. Since we were going back through Moscow the next day, we thought the GAI might arrest us because of our mud-spattered Opel.

I washed my rental car twice a week with the help of my Soviet bucket. "It is illegal to drive a dirty car in the Soviet Union" (Intourist travel guide).

After breakfast we visited Intourist and hired a guide, Irene. She took us around the nearby town of Vladimir and told us about its history. It was settled about 900 years ago and today has a population of 300,000.

We visited the kremlin, with its stone-wall fortification, situated high on the hill overlooking the river. There was an

83

old stone church in the kremlin with carved walls dating back to the thirteenth century. On top of the onion-shaped cupola was a golden crescent in celebration of Russia's victory over the heathen Mongol hordes. One of the churches that we visited was a working Russian Orthodox church. It had a tall golden dome and a series of curved, golden arches outlining the roof. As we walked up to it, we noticed that most of the people walking by stopped, crossed themselves in front of the church, and then proceeded on their way.

"A lot of people are still believers and go to church," admitted Irene, "but not me. In 1977, our constitution was changed to prohibit religious persecution. It is not necessary to be an atheist now to hold a job or get an appointment."

We passed a gymnastics class of four- and five-year-old girls working out on the grassy lawn next to the church. They were wearing leotards and performing a ribbon-twirling routine. Some of the charming little girls were wearing white handkerchiefs or bows in their hair; others were bareheaded. We could imagine that some of them would be performing in the 1992 Olympics.

One of the city's old red-brick churches had been turned into a museum to display the goods produced in the local area. They had beautiful blown glassware and crystal stemware. One display showed the stages of making the enamel jewelry and boxes. The pieces are first given several coats of black enamel. An apprentice then drew the outline of the buildings, people, and animals. The master craftsman takes over at that point and does the delicate finishing work. A finely detailed scene is created on a two-inch round pin. On the second floor of the church, the finely woven laces and bright red needlework were on display. Young Russian women are still taught to do beautiful handwork, which is sold in some village shops.

While in Vladimir, Gloria and I visited the Golden Gates, which were built as the main entrance to the city in the twelfth century. In a room at the top of the gate tower, there is a

We visited a number of "working" churches. "A lot of people are still believers and go to church," our guide admitted. "But not me."

wooden model of the ancient city as it appeared in the thirteenth century. The model depicts a battle between the citizens of Vladimir and the Mongol Tatar hordes. There were thousands of figures and all varieties of weapons being used. The Russians were shown defending their city in a desperate battle. While the theme of the model was very serious, I couldn't help speculating about the stories the Mongols told their wives when they returned from battle:

"Boy, am I glad to get home. My feet are killing me."
"How was your trip, Hon?"
"Don't ask. I can tell you that's the last time we let Chan organize the trip. We sailed up the Volga for three weeks—bad food, no beer, millions of mosquitoes, almost got caught in a forest fire. Finally we came to this lovely little city at the fork of the river. On Sunday morning, we set out for a little old-fashioned looting and burning. The townspeople really got upset. They were shouting at us, throwing spears, dumping hot oil on us, shooting flaming arrows. Logs as big as the tallest trees you've ever seen were hurled down on us. Rocks were dumped, things were pitched, thrown, or shot—everything including the kitchen furniture. All we got for the trouble was a few paintings on some boards and a little gold. Do you think it's easy belonging to the Mongol horde?"

Following our trip around Vladimir, Gloria and I returned to Suzdal, which is known as an open-air museum. Everywhere you go in the city your are within easy reach of the 100 churches, monasteries, convents, and museums. In this town of about 10,000 people, you can walk from one end of the town to the other in twenty minutes, including a stop for an ice-cream cone.

Gloria and I visited an exhibit of old wooden houses and churches. We were particularly interested in the simple wooden houses still used in most of the villages. A lady wearing a traditional Russian dress showed us through a house similar to the ones we had seen along the road between Leningrad and Moscow. There was only one door, always located on the side of the house, and three or four front windows. The front room is the family room, dining room, bedroom, and kitchen. The front right corner of the house contains the religious paintings and family heirlooms and is called the "red corner."

A large, wooden dining table stood in the center of the room with a huge, brass, charcoal-fired samovar sitting in the middle of it. On one wall was a large bed for the parents, and above the bed was a shallow loft for the children to sleep in. On the left of the room was a six-foot–square kitchen with a large, freestanding fireplace-oven. The oven was four or five feet deep and required a special tool, resembling a pitchfork with rollers, to slide the huge pots and pans far back into the oven. There was no sink or running water in the kitchen, only a bucket of water sitting on the bench. Behind the fireplace, the oven extended four or five feet. Straw was placed on top of this section of the oven. The grandparents slept there, since it was the warmest spot in the house.

The Russian stove is a great mass of clay used for both heating and cooking. Because of the great size of the Russian stove, it tends to hold heat well and distribute it hours after the fire has died down. After the flames have died down, the embers and ashes are pushed over to one side. A long rod with one end in the shape of a large U fits about the base of the pots and is used for removing them from the stove. Another long rod, with a hook and lever at one end, is used to remove skillets. The broad wooden shovel device is for loading and unloading loaves of bread. Cooking utensils are large in size and few in number.

The Russian samovar is a self-cooker and a relative new-comer (late eighteenth century) to the Russian household. Following its introduction, it caught on quickly, because the samovar is an economical way to get hot water quickly. A charcoal fire, built in the bottom, heats water surrounding a series of tubes in the body of the samovar. A very strong tea mixture is made in a small teapot that is kept warm on top of the samovar. A small amount of strong tea is poured into a cup and then diluted with hot water from the samovar.

Behind the front room is a work area, near the entryway and outside door. This area can also serve as a spare bedroom. There is a ladder to the attic, which is used for storage. One more small room behind the center rooms was used for storage or as a workroom with the looms and spinning wheel. Often there is a small door leading to the barn or animal shed, which was attached to the back of the house.

Private farming is only done on a small scale, and the area required for storage of equipment and animals is smaller than it used to be. There is also now electricity in the rural homes, which usually means a light bulb hung from the ceiling. Since running water and sewers are uncommon in the country, water is drawn from a community well and outhouses are still fashionable.

The houses in the exhibit area were all made of logs. Along the road from Leningrad to Moscow, only about 10 percent of the houses in the small villages were made of logs. The rest were wooden frame houses made of sawed lumber.

The old monastery in Suzdal is situated in a huge fortification surrounded by a twenty-foot–high brick wall. The only entrance to the two-block square structure is through the fortified gates of a sixty-foot–high tower house. The monastery was used as a fortress whenever the Mongol hordes invaded Suzdal. All the townspeople could live inside the walls for the duration of the invasion. One czar turned the monastery into a political prison at one point in history. Gloria and I toured the prison cells, most of which were four feet by six feet, with no outside windows. Using the monastery as a prison sounded like a diabolical idea until I decided that if I were going to prison, I'd rather have monks as my jailers than underpaid civil servants. From the monastery tower, we could see a white-walled convent about a kilometer away on the other side of the Kamenka River.

"You probably heard that this convent is where Ivan the

The huge Spaso Yevfimiev Monastery in Suzdal is surrounded by a twenty-foot-high brick wall. When the Mongol hordes invaded, all the villages could live inside the walls for the duration of the invasion.

Great sent his first wife after she failed to provide him with an heir," Irene explained. "Ivan got the church's permission to marry again. His second wife bore him a child who would grow up to be Ivan the Terrible. After Ivan's first wife had been in the convent for a long time, there was a rumor that she had become pregnant and borne a son. Ivan the Great sent his servant to the convent to kill the child if the rumor was true.

"When the servant got to the convent, the nuns told him that the baby had died and showed him where he was buried.

A few years ago, when the convent was being repaired, the workmen dug up a small casket. They opened it and found a doll inside dressed in baby clothes. Years after the baby supposedly died, a young man living in this area began to steal from the czar's men and give the money to the peasants, like your Robin Hood. Many people think he was the baby born in the convent," concluded Irene.

Irene related another local custom concerning moving into a new house. The Russians believe that cats have mystical powers. They believe the first occupant of a new house must be a cat. After a house is complete, they open the door and put the cat in. After the cat has gone completely through the house, it is safe for the people to enter. She said this custom still persists today. Her girl friend had just moved into a new apartment. She had borrowed a cat to properly prepare the apartment before she would go in. Sounds as if a rent-a-cat agency might be profitable.

As we left the monastery, we passed a wooden house. I noticed a four-inch–square hole in the logs a few inches above the ground. I explained to Gloria that this vent under the house would allow trapped moisture to escape.

"I'll bet it's a cat door," replied Gloria. About that time, a little yellow kitten stuck its head out of the hole.

Chapter 10
Orel: "No Room—Go to Motel"

Early on Saturday morning, Gloria and I jogged along the river path between the convent and the monastery at Suzdal. The sun was just coming up, and the red-brick monastery walls reflecting on the glass-smooth water made us wonder if the image was real. Downstream a short distance from the convent, a circular pattern of ripples radiated from a Russian woman washing her clothes in the clear stream. We were told that even in the winter, the women come to the frozen river and break the ice to wash clothes.

We had 400 miles to drive today down to Orel, two hundred sixty miles south of Moscow. Since the hotel dining room didn't open until 8:00, we decided to try to get breakfast at one of the food stops along the road. We had passed them every thirty or forty miles on our drive up. The first one we came to was near the village of Vladimir. Since it wasn't quite eight o'clock, the restaurant was still closed. We got to the next one about 8:30. The door was unlocked and the employees were cleaning up from the night before.

"Breakfast?" I asked.

"*Nyet*. Not open," said a burly man in a blue shop coat.

I glanced at the door. The hours for Saturday were posted: "8 A.M. to 8 P.M." "What time do you open?" I asked.

"Whenever we get cleaning done," he snipped back at me.

Gloria and I drove on past another dining room, which was also closed. At 9:30, we saw a tour bus turning into a *stolovaya* (dining room) and followed it.

91

As we followed the Russian tourists into the dining room, Gloria asked, "How come everyone's sitting around drinking beer? I don't see any bacon and eggs."

We got in line behind the busload of tourists and fifteen or twenty minutes later made our way up to the cashier at the beer and bakery counter.

"Eggs?" I asked.

"*Nyet.*"

"Cheese?"

"*Nyet.*"

"Pancakes?"

"*Nyet.*"

"Coffee?"

"*Nyet.*"

"Juice?"

"*Nyet.*"

"Tea?"

"*Da.*"

"Cookies?"

"*Da.*"

I paid for our tea and cookies and waited in the serving line, which wound across one side of the restaurant and down the back. About fifteen minutes later, we got close enough to see what everyone was having for breakfast. The only breakfast being served consisted of rice, a fried meat patty, and cucumbers. We drank our cold tea and ate the cookies and vowed in the future to wait for the hotel dining room to open before undertaking the day's journey.

All along the road to Moscow and south we saw work parties cutting grass. There were groups of ten or twenty men with two-handed scythes and women raking the grass into piles. A tractor or a horse and wagon would come along and pick up the piles of grass to take home to the cows. This seemed to be a popular way to spend a Saturday, since we saw thirty or forty parties that day. Modern and ancient Russia were mixed in these work parties. Even though the day was hot and sunny, the older women were dressed in black stockings, black dresses, and sweaters and had kerchiefs tied around their heads. Dozens of younger women were working alongside the older, dressed only in skimpy bikinis of flaming pink, brilliant orange, fire-engine red, or passionate purple.

While driving through the countryside, we encountered Russian motorists who flashed their lights to warn us of a GAI car ahead. As we rounded the corner, we'd find a GAI car lurking behind the trees by a side road or at the edge of a roadside park. It was interesting to me that in this regimented society where you read about neighbors spying on neighbors, the average person would go to the trouble (and risk) of warning his fellow motorist about the traffic cop. I guess that is just a part of the universal spirit of comradery in outmaneuvering the authorities. And it really accomplishes the police's objective by causing people to slow down and drive more cautiously.

Gloria and I obtained a crude street map of Orel in advance so that we could find our Intourist Hotel—the Rossiya. The map of the city showed only three main streets, which should have been sufficient for us to get oriented to the general area. We entered this industrial town of a quarter-million people, followed Main Street, crossed the bridge, and were right on course, looking for October Street, which should have led off to the right. At that point, Main Street ran out. The entire eight lanes of Main Street were torn up so the trolley tracks could be repaired. Orel is a river town and streets do not run parallel to one another, so we couldn't simply move over one street and bypass the construction. We stopped and asked the local policeman for directions. He gave us one of those comedy routines: "Go back eight blocks, turn left at the gas station, go four blocks, turn left at the church, go ten blocks, turn right at the yellow house, go four blocks, turn left at the twin birch trees, go straight . . . "—all in Russian.

The rain was pouring down in sheets. I turned the car around and started wandering through town. We followed the directions as best we could, and to our surprise we spotted the Rossiya about two blocks down a one-way, do-not-enter, street. We circled, got onto the street going in the right direction, and finally pulled up to the side of the hotel. I dashed in the entryway through a torrential downpour and handed our documents to the receptionist. She studied them for a few minutes and then announced, "No room. You go to Shipka Motel."

"But my tourist card says the Rossiya."

"You go to Shipka Motel."

"Where is that?"

"Back toward Moscow."

"But Intourist told me the Rossiya."

"No room. You go to Shipka Motel."

I walked back to the car and retraced our trail to Main Street. At about seven o'clock we finally arrived at the Shipka Motel. We went in and located the Intourist desk.

"Why do we have to stay here rather than at the Rossiya?" I asked the receptionist.

"Telegram from Moscow Intourist. There are changes in your itinerary."

"Oh!"

I read the telegram. They had turned our itinerary around and now had us traveling to the next four cities in reverse order. That was no problem, since the order of the itinerary was arbitrary, but in the shuffle we were scheduled for only one night in Odessa on the Black Sea rather than the two we had originally planned. Also, on the last day, instead of being within twenty miles of the Russian/Hungarian border and able to get to customs early in the morning, we were 400 miles away and could not arrive at the border until late afternoon.

"Why the change?" I asked.

"Don't know. You ask Intourist in Kiev."

"Why did they change things?" Gloria asked me.

"Moscow probably thought things were going too smoothly and wanted to add a little adventure," I answered.

Once we were in our room, I said to Gloria, "I'm going to take a hot bath and try to relax. Twelve hours of driving today has done me in."

My next surprise was the bathtub. I've seen many different styles of bathtubs during my travels, but this one was new to me. It was built in the shape of a throne, with a place to sit and lower section to soak your feet. I filled it nearly full of hot water and climbed in. The water level only came to my belly button. I tried to lie down, but the edge of the seat section caught me in the middle of my back. By doubling up, I could get down in the deep end so that the water covered me, but my knees were then under my armpits. I didn't soak and relax very long. The bath was interrupted by a knock at the door. Gloria was already deep into her nap, so I wound a towel around me and cautiously opened the door a half-inch or so to peer out.

"Are you American?" asked a young couple standing in the hall wearing USC T-shirts.

"Yes. From Ohio."

"Great! We saw your name on the register. We're from California. Would you like to have dinner with us?"

"Okay. How about 8:00? We'll meet in the dining room."

We approached the dining room a few minutes early in order to try to locate our new American friends. The hostess asked us what country we were from.

"America."

She escorted us to a table for two with an American flag perched in the middle.

"We'd like to eat with our friends," I told her, pointing

95

to the Californian couple, whom she had already seated at another table for two.

"No," she said. "Can't move table."

"We'll sit at another table. They can join us."

After a little negotiation, we finally got the entire matter altered to our satisfaction and the four of us were sitting together. Tom and Beverly were from Los Angeles. They had been traveling for about a year.

"Quit our jobs, sold our house, and simply took off. Our parents think we're crazy. We plan to travel around the world for three or four years and then go home and raise a family," Tom said.

"We bought a VW camper in Germany and have traveled through most of the southern European countries, Egypt, and the eastern European countries. We plan to spend a month or two in the Soviet Union, then drive through Scandinavia for a few months," Beverly continued.

Their plans included driving through Africa, Australia, and South America. They had another two years and fifty thousand miles to go. Now that's an ambitious and courageous adventure!

We ordered supper, and the waitress asked if we planned to have breakfast in the dining room tomorrow morning.

"Yes," I told her.

"What time?"

"About eight o'clock."

"What would you like? Eggs, coffee, bacon, juice?"

"Juice, eggs, cheese, and coffee."

This was the first time a waitress had ever taken our breakfast order at suppertime. They have strange ways in the Soviet Union.

After supper, we headed back to our room. In the evening, Gloria usually read while I wrote for a while. Then we would spend some time planning the route for the next day and getting the maps straightened out. It was dark when we went down the hall to our room, so dark that it was impossible to read the room numbers.

"Why is it so dark?" I asked the key lady.

"Storm. No lights," she said.

We had to feel the numbers on the doors in order to find our room. Once in the room, I took the flashlight from my briefcase so that we could brush our teeth. There was no reading, writing, or planning that night. At ten o'clock, the power was still off. Everything was still in blackness.

Chapter 11
Kiev: *"Nyet Benzina"*

"Today we'll leave the republic of Russia and drive into the Ukrainian breadbasket," I told Gloria as we headed for Kiev on Sunday.

"The Ukrainian breadbasket?"

"The farmlands of the Soviet Union."

"Oh."

The countryside was rolling farmland and looked much like Kentucky. The two-lane roads were lined with purple flowers and wild red poppies. There were large herds of brown cows tended by Ukrainian cowboys on horseback. They carried long, braided whips, but were dressed in normal rural work clothes, consisting of boots, trousers, and suit jackets—no special costumes like the North American cowboys or Argentinian gauchos. For the next hundred miles, the land flattened out like northern Illinois. There was lots of wheat, some corn, and a few pine or birch forests. We had had little or no trouble getting gas during the previous ten days of the trip. Today I let the gas tank get lower than usual before pulling into a benzine station a hundred miles from Kiev.

"Why do they have the hoses wrapped around the gas pumps like that?" Gloria asked.

"I don't know," I said.

I pulled up behind ten cars parked by the pumps. There was a crowd of people gathered around the office and a loud discussion going on. About that time, the attendant pulled out a card and stuck it in the window. "NYET BENZINA."

"That's probably why the hoses are wrapped around the pump," I said to Gloria. "No problem. We still have enough gas to get to the next station," I assured her. As we pulled out of the station, I noticed a GAI standing nearby. He waved his baton for me to pull over.

"Hello," he said in Russian. "Documents, please."

I gave him our tourist card, passports, and visas. He went to the back of the car, looked it over, and studied our documents.

"Where is the car from?" he asked.

"Denmark," I said, pointing to my DK sticker on the trunk. Only the sticker wasn't there anymore. ("It is against the law to drive a foreign car in the Soviet Union unless it prominently displays an international sticker, indicating the country of origin."—*Intourist Motoring Guide*.)

I quickly wrote "DK" in the dust on the trunk, but he didn't think that was sufficient or humorous.

"Where is the decal?" he demanded.

"Gone! It was right there yesterday, but it's gone now," I said.

"Show me car documents," he persisted.

I got out the car registration, green insurance card, and rental contract. He checked the license number, engine number, and body number before he handed the documents back to me.

"You check with Intourist in Kiev and get decal," he ordered.

"I didn't tell him, but I seriously doubt if there is a DK decal in all the Soviet Union," I confided to Gloria as we drove away.

"Are we going to run out of gas before we get to a benzine station?"

"Should be a gas station in the next town, about twenty miles down the road," I told her. Wrong! The next gas station

99

was seventy miles away. We drove slowly and tried not to breathe in order to improve the gas mileage. The gauge was on "empty" when we finally saw the benzine station ahead.

As we pulled into the station, I noticed the cars and trucks parked at odd angles around the pumps and most of the hoses were either wrapped around the pumps or lying on the ground. There was a noisy crowd of drivers gathered around the office shouting at the attendant and each other. The attendant had just put up a sign in the window: "NO 72, 76, 95, or 98 BENZIN."

"Do you think we can push the car the remaining thirty miles to Kiev?" I asked Gloria.

"That's not funny. Ask the lady where the nearest benzine station is," she replied.

I went up to the office and asked.

"What octane you want?" she asked through the little porthole in the office window.

"Ninety-three or ninety-eight," I said.

"Give me coupon," she demanded.

I slid two ten-liter coupons through the window to her. She motioned me to the ninety-three octane Pump Number 10, the only one still working in the station. I got back in the car and lined up behind ten or fifteen other cars. I sat there and thought of the ice-cream stands in Moscow. They always ran out of ice cream just before we got our turn. As the car in front of me finished filling up, I took the hose and said a little prayer. Fortunately, there was enough benzine for me to get twenty liters, which would get us to Kiev.

"I'll never let the tank get that low again, not below half full," I promised Gloria as we drove away from the benzine station.

Kiev, which is approximately 500 miles southwest of Moscow, currently has a population of around 2 million people. I had two maps of the city, one a large-scale map that gave no indication as to where we should enter the city. The other was a small-scale one that showed our hotel, but no indication how to get there from the highway on which we were driving. I took a wild guess and drove through the residential area. The first major street led downtown. It turned out to be the street on which our hotel was located. We arrived at the hotel in record time. I checked with Intourist, and there the receptionist informed me that we were staying at a different hotel.

"Only tour groups in this hotel."

"But Moscow knew we were not a tour group. Why did they tell us five days ago we would be here at the Dnieper?"

"Don't know. You are staying at the Lybed. Go down the street four blocks, turn right, go about a mile. Hotel on left."

It was four o'clock when we left the Hotel Dnieper for the Lybed. I found the turn in five or six minutes. The hotel was on the left, right alongside the no–left-turn sign. Okay. We'd go straight and then circle back. Forty-five minutes later, we were still trying to find a way back to the Lybed Hotel. We had gotten on a one-way street that went for four miles without a turnoff except into apartment complexes. We finally got back to the hotel area and made three passes before we arrived at the front door. After we got our room, I stopped at the Intourist desk to find out why our itinerary had been changed.

"Why did Moscow change our itinerary?" I asked the receptionist as I handed her my original itinerary and the telegram from Moscow.

"Ah," she said as she read the telegram. She shook her head and called another Intourist person over.

"Why did Moscow change our itinerary?" I asked the second lady.

She looked over the itinerary and the telegram. "I don't know," she said, "but I will call the supervisor."

"The Intourist agent at Orel told me you would be able

to explain why Moscow changed our itinerary," I said to the supervisor.

"Ah, yes," she said. "I thought you had requested the change when I received a copy of the telegram from Moscow."

"Me? Request a change! No. They messed things up on this new itinerary. We have only one night in Odessa, and we'll be 400 miles away from the border on the day we plan to leave the Soviet Union. How can it be changed back?"

"Impossible," she said.

"Could you send a telegram to Moscow and ask why they changed our itinerary and if we could change it back?"

"Impossible," she repeated.

"But they have made a mistake," I said.

"Exactly what would you like to do?"

"At a minimum, we would like to cut off one day at Chernovtsy and add back our overnight stay at Uzhgorod, near the Soviet border."

"No problem," she said with a big smile. "When you get to Chernovtsy, ask them to shorten your itinerary. We do it all the time. No problem."

"Okay. But let's do it now, from here, so that we can change the dates of arrival at the other five cities after Chernovtsy."

"Impossible! Your problem is not in Kiev. It is in Chernovtsy. When you get to Chernovtsy, you make the change."

"Our problem is in Moscow. We would like to get it straightened out before we get to Chernovtsy. I'm afraid they will tell us, oh, you should have made the change in Kiev or Orel or anywhere besides Chernovtsy."

It is difficult to argue with Intourist. They never say no; they just put you off. Either you go away, or the problem goes away. Gloria and I figured we might as well enjoy Kiev while we were here and worry about the itinerary when we got to Chernovtsy.

After supper, I curled up with the Intourist guide to absorb the history of the Kiev area:

The site of Kiev has been occupied for fifty thousand years by a kaleidoscopic collection of nomadic tribes. The first of whom we have much knowledge are the Scythians. They held sway in southern Russia as early as 700 B.C. The Greek historian Herodotus, who visited Scythia in 500 B.C., reported that they drank the blood of their enemies, scalped them, and sewed the scalps together to make cloaks for themselves. They also took vapor baths, throwing hemp seed on red-hot stones to produce vapor, "for they never," adds Herodotus, "by any chance wash their bodies with water."

In the third century A.D. the Goths poured into South Russia from the northwest, only to be driven out a century or two later by the Huns, a tribe of Turkish or Mongolian origin.

It was not until the ninth century that signs of a more settled population appeared. This was the moment most historians pick for the beginning of modern Russian history.

The tribe that settled on the fertile plains around Kiev and turned to agriculture was the Eastern Slavs. The Slavs, who had lived in the Northern Carpathians under the rule of the Huns for centuries, started to gradually split up in the fifth century. The Western Slavs became the Poles, Czechs, or Slovaks, the Southern Slavs pushed down into the Balkan Peninsula and became the Serbs, Croats and Slovenes, and the Eastern Slavs, who remained roughly where they were, became Russians.

The settlers around Kiev began to see that a good living could be made in trade. Kiev developed on the great river trade route between Scandinavia and the Byzantine. From a mere trading center Kiev grew into a prosperous city. The early Slavic inhabitants were gradually absorbed by the Varengians (Vikings) in the ninth century. In A.D. 882, the Viking prince Oleg became ruler of the area from Novgorod to Kiev. Kiev quickly became the capital of the Russian empire, and the city prospered. After Oleg's death, his wife, Olga, ruled

Kiev and instituted a number of much needed reforms. Following one of her pilgrimages to Constantinopole, she decided to give up her pagan beliefs and accept Christianity.

It was Olga's grandson Vladimir who consolidated the confederation of principalities into a tight-knit Kievan Russia. In 988, Vladimir dismissed his large harem and organized the general baptism of his subjects in the Dnieper. He accepted the Eastern Orthodox Christianity of the Byzantine rather than the Western Catholic religion. With Christianity came literacy and the Cyrillic alphabet, devised by Saint Cyril and his brother Methodius.

Following Vladimir's death, the country continued to prosper under the leadership of Yaroslav and his son Vladimir Monomath. During the twelth century the power of Kiev started to decline, with the rise of importance of Suzdal and Novgorod. In 1240, Kiev was overrun by the Mongol Tatars and burned and plundered. During the next four centuries, Kiev was repeatedly sacked and occupied by the Mongols, Lithuanians, and Poles. The town dwindled from a powerful capital of Kievan Russia to an unpretentious village with a few thousand inhabitants.

In the seventeenth century, a renaissance began, with Kiev becoming the center of the Ukrainian nation. In a war of liberation (1658–59), the Ukrainians with the support of the Cossacks, broke away from Poland. In 1667, they were annexed back into Russia. They redeveloped their position in trade and established a thriving industrial base in Kiev. By the beginning of the nineteenth century, Kiev had grown to 30,000 inhabitants and taken its place among the leading cities of the Empire. Kiev continued to grow and prosper into the 20th century.

Following the 1917 overthrow of the czar, a Ukrainian Socialist Republic was formed. A bitter civil war raged in Kiev for the next three years while the Ukrainian Nationalist, Bolshevik, German, and Polish armies tried to wrestle control. Finally, in 1920 the Nationalists were successful. In 1922, the Ukraine became one of the four original republics that formed the Soviet Union. In 1934, Kiev regained the role of capital of the Ukraine.

During the Second World War, Kiev was occupied by the Nazis, for two years. During that time, the city was systematically destroyed and 300,000 of its population killed or deported. But once the occupation was ended, Kiev's resiliency allowed it to spring back to life as it had a hundred times before.

In the morning, I tried to decide what to do about the missing decal. There was not a single DK decal to be bought in all the Ukraine. I did the next best thing. I drew the DK letters on a piece of hotel stationery, cut the circle out, and pasted it inside the rear window of the car.

After breakfast, we headed for the collective market, or farmers' market, near the center of the city. Every family in the Soviet Union is guaranteed a small piece of land on which to grow products for their own use or for sale. These small private plots of land amount to only about 1 percent of the cultivated land, but they account for about half of the fruits and vegetables produced in the Soviet Union. Food, as well as other products in this country, is sold by the State at a predetermined price. However, in these farmers' markets you are allowed to charge whatever the market will bear— capitalism at its best. The fruits and vegetables are plump, clean, and neatly arranged in an attractive display. On our previous trip to Kiev in November 1974, we bought some beautiful apples at the farmers' market. On the current trip, there had been no fruit to be seen since we entered Leningrad. We were anxious to see if we could get apples in the Kiev market.

"No. Not in season," we were told. "Only local fruit is sold here."

There are no refrigeration or transport facilities available to bring the ripe fruit from the southern republics. We bought two quarts of sweet, juicy strawberries grown locally from one of the market stalls.

"If you eat any more strawberries, you are going to turn

Every family in the Soviet Union is guaranteed a small plot of land to grow produce for their own use. These plots, which amount to only 1 percent of the cultivated land, account for about half of the fresh vegetables.

into one," I told Gloria as she finished off a quart of berries.

"That's okay," she said. "Medical service is free here, even for tourists."

Americans don't realize how much information they absorb in a normal day—newspapers, letters, memos, magazines, TV, radio. They get hooked on obtaining information in large amounts on a daily basis. Giving up that information input is like quitting smoking cold turkey. Gloria and I hadn't brought any reading material with us. After two weeks of trying to find something to read in English, we were getting desperate. We visited a dozen kiosks looking for magazines,

The farmers' markets are capitalism at its best. The fruit and vegetables are plump, clean, and neatly displayed.

newspapers, anything in English. No luck. One night, out of desperation I decided to read the maintenance manual for the rental car. I read it cover to cover in fifteen minutes. Then I looked around for more to read. There was one page of emergency fire instructions in English in the hotel room. I read those twice. That was enough to satisfy me for that evening. In the morning, we visited a number of bookstores and finally found some English-language paperbacks, including a copy of Isaac Asimov's *I Robot*. I rationed my reading and set up a schedule so that the books would hold out for the rest of the trip. Two chapters a day and those books would last until we got out of the Soviet Union, maybe even until we got back to Copenhagen.

During the stay in Kiev, we watched some Soviet TV to compare it with U.S. TV. The morning program was an exercise class. In the early afternoon, they presented cultural programs such as ballets, operas, or plays. There was a presentation of the Red Army Chorus singing and dancing. In the evening, it was usually World War II movies. I went to the lounge and sat with the key lady and some other guests to watch the Monday-night movie with no commercials.

It was a war movie that was set in Russia during 1943. The opening scene showed twenty or thirty Russian soldiers sloshing through mud and rain. The central figure was a young Russian officer. Through the action and a few recognizable Russian words, I was able to follow the story. The soldiers marched all night and overran a German position on the hill. In the morning, the Germans counterattacked and drove the Russians back. That evening, the Russians rallied and recaptured the hill. The young officer became a hero by the end of the movie. After that movie, another one started with the same characters and setting, only two years later. I couldn't force myself to watch the sequel.

While in Kiev, I made the mistake of referring to someone from Kiev as a Russian. I got a lecture on the fact that "Russia" is not interchangeable with "Soviet Union" or "USSR." Russia is one of the fifteen republics in the Soviet Union. Each of these fifteen republics has its own language, customs, and history. Kiev is in the republic of the Ukraine. The language is Ukrainian, which is different from Russian. As a matter of fact, the Ukrainians study Russian in school as a foreign language. I was told that calling someone from Kiev a Russian is like calling someone from Ireland an Englishman. You'll get a nasty glance at least and probably some harsh words and a lecture on Ukrainian history.

In each town that we visited, we wandered through various food stores to see how people in the Soviet Union do their daily shopping. The procedure is a little more complicated than simply driving your station wagon up to the nearest supermarket.

The women have to shop on a daily basis, because there is a minimum of refrigeration and freezing is unheard of in the average Russian home. For bread, it's necessary to go to a bread store. The bread store contains forty or fifty trays of breads in various shapes and sizes stacked against the wall. The fresh-baked black, brown, and white breads give off a delicious odor designed to make you buy more than you originally intended. There is a freshness fork hanging on a piece of twine by each stack of trays.

"Too dry—overbaked," commented an ample Russian woman as she jabbed a loaf of black bread. "Too doughy—not cooked enough," she observed as the fork came out of another loaf with bits of dough stuck to it. "Ah." She beamed. "Just right." Like Goldilocks, she had found a loaf that suited her.

The unsliced loaves are carried to the cashier, where you pay the equavalent of twenty-five or fifty cents, depending on the size and type of bread selected. Each shopper brings his or her own shopping bag to carry the unwrapped loaves.

For sour cream, yogurt, butter, cheese, or eggs, the Russians must go to the milk-products store. There are always long lines at the various counters. Each day, I usually bought some cheese so that we could stop along the road for a picnic lunch. As I stood in the cheese line, the lady in front of me turned around and asked me to hold her place in line. She took her crockery jar over to the sour-cream counter, got it filled, and was back in the cheese line before it had moved two feet. I noticed the lady in front of her dart over and get her butter and then come back to the cheese line. As this continued, with people running to get eggs and coming back, I realized why the cheese line moved so slowly. Everyone in the store had a place reserved in the cheese line. While it moved up, they were able to complete the rest of their shopping in the store.

Canned goods are sold in the canned-goods store. The normal shop isn't very large, since there is not much variety or quantity in stock in the Russian stores. Usually there were glass jars with one or two kinds of beans, tomatoes, peas, and pickled cucumbers. All the glass jars are returnable. We seldom saw any cans of food unless they were from Hungary or Czechoslovakia.

To obtain fresh vegetables, it is necessary to go to a green market. This time of year, there were potatoes, beets, cabbage, carrots, cucumbers, and strawberries available.

If a shopper has any time, energy, or money left, she might go to a meat market. The meat-market floor is always cold and wet. The store has a strong fishy odor coming from four or five varieties of fresh fish laid out for inspection. The supply of meat was minimal, with most of the showcase taken up by fish or poultry.

The beer store is a must for the daily shopper. It contains bottled beer, wine, and nectar. A stop at the confectioner's shop to pick up some cookies and sweets after a day's shopping brings the grand total of shopping hours to a record two hours and fifteen minutes. It is difficult to understand how Soviet people put on weight, with all the running around they do.

We talked to a lady in Kiev about the different types of jobs available and how they are regarded. To our surprise, the street sweeper's job is considered a plum. It pays well; the hours are short. The ladies are out on the streets at five or six o'clock in the morning and are finished sweeping by nine or ten. Another desirable job is that of trolley driver. It pays as well as an engineering job, and has a lot fewer headaches.

We had visited at least fifteen cities in the Soviet Union from Leningrad to Yalta. There was something missing in each of these cities—a pizza shop! We have eaten pizza in every other country we've visited, including Japan, Thailand, and Tahiti. But there are no pizza places in the Soviet Union. I wonder how much a Soviet franchise for a Pizza Hut would cost.

Chapter 12
Vinnitsa: The Original Road

Vinnitsa, which is 150 miles southwest of Kiev in the central Ukraine, is known for sugar beets and Dr. Pirogov, who developed the technique of extracting blood plasma. The countryside between Kiev and Vinnitsa varies from flat fields of wheat to small, rolling hills of sugar beets or meadows. On the outskirts of Vinnitsa, a town of almost a quarter-million people, we had to dodge wagons loaded with sugar beets coming in from the fields and wagons full of loose sugar driving from the refineries to the bagging plant. As soon as we found our hotel, I contacted Intourist to find out if they knew why Moscow had changed our itinerary.

"Very interesting question," replied the Intourist clerk. "I was wondering the same thing myself."

"Can you help me find out why or even how to get it changed back?"

"No. You can probably do that in Chernovtsy, but not here."

We hired an Intourist guide to show us around the town. It took about forty-five minutes for the Intourist people to fill out the paperwork for the standard city tour and get the authorizing stamps and approvals. I asked our guide, Dimitri, why it took so long.

"Oh, that's not long," he said. "It took over four hours yesterday."

As we walked out of the Intourist office, Dimitri offered us a short history of his city:

"Vinnitsa began as a fortress town on the bank of the Bug River in the fourteenth century. The area, at that time, was under the control of Lithuanians. In 1569, the city came under the control of Poland. Many new churches and monasteries were built in Vinnitsa during the Polish occupation. At the end of the eighteenth century, Vinnitsa became part of Ukrainian Russia. Prior to the 1917 Revolution, the city was mainly a trading center with small handcrafts and food industries. Following the Revolution, it developed rapidly into an industrial center and important railroad junction. During World War Two, there was violent fighting in the town, which was occupied by the Nazis from 1941 to 1944."

Next, Dimitri took us to see where the most famous Vinnitsian, Dr. Pirogov, lived and died. It was a beautiful estate on the edge of town, with a tree-lined lane, its own church, and a beautiful garden surrounding the ten-room mansion. When we got to the front porch of the house, the attendant informed us we would have to put on slippers over our shoes to avoid scratching the wooden floors. They had placed four chairs by the door so that you could sit down to tie the slippers around your shoes. A large calico cat was asleep on the red velvet cushion of one of the chairs. The other chairs were occupied by some Russian students taking the house tour. We stood on one foot and then the other to get our slippers on.

"Must be the owner," said Gloria as she put another star on her cat count calendar.

"Dr. Pirogov did a lot of work on the battlefields of the nineteenth century," explained Dimitri as we walked through the house. "He developed the technique for making blood plasma. He also developed many of the surgical instruments still used today."

We passed a number of exhibits, pictures, and posters of bone saws, surgical clamps, and scalpels that illustrated aspects of Dr. Pirogov's career.

113

"He treated all the local peasants and never charged them anything," Dimitri continued. "The townspeople loved him. Perhaps one of his more famous claims to fame is the embalming process that he developed. This process was used to preserve the body of Lenin and later that of Stalin. Dr. Pirogov's body is embalmed by the same process and can be seen in the church in the back of this house. I wanted to take you there, but unfortunately it is closed. We got such a late start for our tour."

On the outskirts of Vinnitsa, Dimitri showed us a new suburb that provided housing for 100,000 people. It consisted of a square mile of apartment buildings, schools, and shops, all built as a planned city. Several technical institutes were built into the complex, along with beauty shops, bakeries, child-care centers, grocery stores, and everything required for a self-contained city. Dimitri next took us to the old part of Vinnitsa, dating back to the thirteenth century.

"This church dates back to the thirteenth or fourteenth century," he explained as we bounced over a cobblestone road that nearly jarred the fillings out of our teeth.

"Would you believe," he said proudly, "that this is part of the original road of Vinnitsa?"

"Yes-s-s, I'd-d-d belie-e-e-ve it-t-t," stuttered Gloria as she bounced all over the backseat of the car.

At the hotel, we talked with some teachers about the education system in the Soviet Union. They explained that the children start school at age seven and attend school for ten years. They can go on to a technical institute, teachers' college, or a vocational school if desired. If they choose vocational training, they start that right after their eighth year of schooling. The technical institutes have a five-year curriculum. The students are given free room and board plus a small allowance, depending upon their individual needs and grades. The teachers told us that the allowance may run from the equi-

114

valent of forty dollars to eighty dollars per month. To get into the institute, a series of examinations is required so applicants can complete for the available openings. The foreign-language department in the institute is one of the most difficult to enter. There may be ten or twenty applicants for every opening. In contrast, the mathematics department is not able to fill its quota. Requirements have been lowered and allowances increased to attract applicants. After a student finishes at the institute, he is required to serve for three years in a job and location chosen by the committee, to repay the system for the schooling. After that, the student is free to take the job of his choice, assuming that an opening is available.

When we got back to the hotel, we picked up our room key and headed up the stairs. We'd seen a variety of keys in our various Soviet hotels. Sometimes the keys were large enough to fit a castle door. One key was flat, with the mechanism sticking out about one-half an inch on each side, but the key in Vinnitsa was most unique. I couldn't figure out how it worked. I had to have the lady who watches the floor help me. It was perfectly round, like an ice pick, and about that size. It had five grooves cut into the top side on a forty-five degree diagonal. The key was inserted into a small, round hole in the door. The front part picked up the first tooth of the mechanism and caused the bolt to start sliding back. Each additional groove picked up a new tooth and forced the bolt back farther, sort of like a worm gear. Quite an unusual key!

Chapter 13
Chernovtsy: "You Must Speak to the Director"

From Vinnitsa, we headed south to the Rumanian border and the Ukrainian city of Chernovtsy. We passed into rolling countryside where herds of cows stood silhouetted on tops of hills. In some areas, the raging streams had eaten away the hillside, exposing sheer cliffs of limestone. In a defiant gesture, the villagers built their stucco-covered tile homes right up to the edge of the cliffs. One step out the back door and whoosh . . .

In Chernovtsy, a border town of 200,000 people, it was necessary to contact Intourist again to see if we could readjust our itinerary to allow us to spend the last night near the Soviet border. At the Intourist Service Bureau, I explained our problem to Nina.

"Someone made a mistake when they changed our itinerary. We can't drive 600 kilometers on the last day and get through customs. We must stay closer to the border. We only want to spend one night in Chernovtsy and add a stop at Uzhgorod as originally planned."

"I can't make the changes," Nina said.

"Well, who can?"

"You must speak to the director."

"May I see him now?"

"No. He isn't here."

"When will he be back?"

"I think in two hours or maybe tomorrow," she said uncertainly.

"I can't wait until tommorrow," I said.

"You come back at 5:30. We'll see," she said.

To soothe my jangled nerves, Gloria and I took a long walk around the town. As Chernovtsy was a border town, there were a lot of Rumanian tourists hurrying from shop to shop buying vodka, Russian dolls, and other souvenirs. In the center of Chernovtsy is a shopping street that has been blocked off to car traffic and turned into a walking street. This shopping mall is lined with souvenir shops, food stores, and clothing shops and stretches four or five blocks. It's a narrow brick street with the bricks arranged in an artistic fan or petal pattern. Along the streets were pushcarts selling fresh flowers, and on every corner there was an ice-cream vendor. The whole place was mass confusion with tourists elbow-to-elbow carrying their purchases in string bags. At 5:30, we returned to Intourist to see if the director had shown up.

"The director is not here, but I have sent a telegram to your next stop, at Kishinev. They are expecting you tomorrow as you requested," Nina said.

"And what about the arrangements at the remaining cities along the way?" I asked.

"We can only deal with one city at a time. You will have to contact the remaining cities as you proceed on your trip."

"You mean that every day we have to contact Intourist and see if they can change the next city, one city at a time?"

"That is right. That is the way it is done."

We thanked Nina for her help and headed to the hotel restaurant for supper.

"This one-day-at-a-time game seems to be designed to prolong the suspense," I said to Gloria.

When we got to the restaurant, there was a "Closed" sign on the door. I stuck my head in, and three or four people were setting the tables and placing salads and appetizers around.

"What time do you open?" I asked one of the waiters.

117

"*Nyet obeda* [no supper]," he snapped, pointing to the sign.

Apparently they were setting up for a group and were not planning to serve individuals. We wandered upstairs and started searching for the buffet that was supposed to be on each floor.

"It must be this unmarked door," said Gloria after we had wandered around the entire floor twice.

I opened the door gingerly and peeked in. "You're right. This is it."

We went in and checked the menu. Cold sausage, biscuits, and beer were about all that was left. While we were trying to make up our minds, two more people came in. That must have been the capacity for the buffet, because the lady running the place went over and locked the door. We got our sausage and beer and stood up at the small round table to eat our gourmet's delight. When we left, the lady opened the door again to let another couple in.

After supper, I read up on the history of the city from the Intourist guide before going to bed.

First mentions of Chernovtsy were early in the fifteenth century. The town developed in the foothill region of the Carpathian Mountains and is situated on the Prut River. While serving as a customs town for Moldavia, it was frequently plundered by the Turks and the Poles. It was under the control of Turkey until 1768, when it was taken by the Russians. Seven years later, in 1775, it became part of Austria and was renamed Czernowitz. Under Austrian rule it prospered and grew in importance as an industrial center of the Bukovina region. In 1916 it was again occupied by Russian troops. During the turmoil of the revolution it became Rumanian and remained so until 1940, when it was ceded back to Russia. It was occupied by Rumanian troops from 1941 to 1944 and severely damaged.

For breakfast we went back down to the hotel restaurant. We cautiously peeked in to see if we were allowed. The waitress signaled an "all's clear," and we took a table by the window.

"What'll you have?" I asked Gloria. "More sausage and beer?"

"Why don't we take pot luck and order the *komplekt*?"

"Okay," I agreed.

"A number one for me and a number two for my wife," I explained to the waitress.

"What's a number one?" asked Gloria.

"I'm not sure, but it'll probably be good," I said.

Gloria got apple juice, two slices of beef, a sweet roll with butter, *bliny* filled with cheese curd and covered with sour cream, plus black coffee.

"Now this is all right," she said approvingly.

"You'd better wait until you see mine," I said. "It'll be even better."

The waitress returned with her tray and set my yogurt, black bread, fried liver and onions, barley, dill pickle, and tea down.

"Want to trade?" I asked.

"Not on your life," laughed Gloria as she speared her Russian pancakes.

119

Chapter 14
Kishinev: Moldavian Speed Trap

On Wednesday, we entered Moldavia and drove to the capital city of Kishinev, 300 miles south of Kiev. Moldavia is one of the fifteen Soviet republics and is situated on the southern border of the USSR, just above Rumania. The villages in this area are larger than in the northern part of the country. We learned that, due to the moderate Mediterranean climate and good black soil, it is a very desirable place to live. The population density of Moldavia is 115 people per square kilometer, the highest of any republic in the USSR and, in fact, equal to that of Denmark.

Moldavia is a favorite nesting place of the stork. Moldavian wine made from the plump grapes grown on the warm, rolling hillsides was sold in bottles with a trademark of a white stork holding a bunch of grapes in its beak on the label. As we drove by the large, shallow lakes, we often saw storks wading and fishing for their supper. Numerous telephone poles were crowned with a huge nest of sticks and a long-legged stork perched on the crossbeam.

As we rounded the corner and came in sight of one of the rest stops, Gloria let out a shriek of surprise. "That's the biggest bird I've ever seen."

At the edge of the rest stop stood a twenty-five–foot-high stork and an eight-foot-high water pitcher. From the stork's beak dangled a long rope with a bucket on the end. If you pulled on the rope, the stork tilted over to drink from the pitcher. At the same time, the rope and bucket dropped down into a well. When you let go, the stork pulled up a bucket of clear, cool well water. We stopped to sample the water and take a picture of the giant stork.

The shallow lakes of Moldavia are favorite feeding grounds for the storks. One rest stop there boasted a twenty-five–foot-high bird with a water pail hung from its beak.

We saw a lot of machinery in the fields of Moldavia, especially the larger caterpillar-type tractors plowing. However, much of the farming is still done by hand. We passed wheat fields with workers cutting wheat by hand and stacking it in neat sheaves as they have done for hundreds of years. In one large field, there were forty or fifty people, wielding hand scythes, cutting the hay. Another thirty or forty raked it into piles while four or five teams of horses dragged the piles to a central place to be stacked. In the beet fields, teams of people were hoeing the weeds along the rows. When we saw caterpillar-tractors plowing, there were usually groups of ten or fifteen people following the plow with hoes to break up the clods of dirt.

The houses in the southern Ukraine and in Moldavia changed from wood or log to stone or brick. One reason is the lack of trees in the area. Another factor is the coolness provided by the stone.

We noticed that the Soviet Union is progressive in women's rights and equality. In one town, our hotel was being renovated, and we watched as women carried fifty-pound bags of plaster and cement up the stairs to the fourth floor. Along the highway, we saw road gangs of women digging up the highway and shoveling hot asphalt from the trucks. In the towns, we often encountered women unloading cases of beer from trucks and lugging them into shops. With the shortage of men in the Soviet Union due to heavy losses in the Second World War, women have taken over jobs once reserved for men.

As we got farther into Moldavia, we saw the countryside getting hillier, resembling the landscape of Pennsylvania. The land is almost 100 percent cultivated, with grape arbors, beet fields, and orchards.

Near Kishinev, the two-lane highway widened to a four-lane, divided highway. We were cruising along at eighty kilometers an hour with the rest of the traffic when I noticed a bus driver in the right lane waving to me. That's not unusual here. A lot of people wave at foreign cars because they see so few of them, so I waved back. When I saw a frantic look on the bus driver's face, I knew something was wrong. I looked ahead and could just barely make out the yellow fender of the GAI car sticking out from behind the tree. Two GAI officers stepped out and signaled for me to pull over. We had fallen into a Moldavian speed trap! I pulled over and got our out travel documents.

"*Bystro egete* [Going too fast]," said the officer, waving his arms dramatically to emphasize the point. I hadn't seen a village, a sign, or any other indication of houses marking this part of the road as a town or residential area. But apparently we were in a residential area, and the speed limit in those areas is 60 kilometers per hour. I offered no excuses, just listened to the lecture and waited to see if Gloria and I would be taken to jail. He looked over our documents and decided to write a warning on our tourist card. He wrote: "The driver was proceeding at an excessive speed of 80 kilometers per hour in a residential zone. He was warned to observe the speed limit." The GAI then signed the tourist card. The officer courteously warned me against a second offense, tipped his hat, and told me we could go. We drove the remaining fifteen miles at 60 kilometers an hour, even in the 90-kilometer speed zone.

Kishinev is a city of half a million people, about one-eighth the population of the entire republic. It consists of an uptown (old section) and downtown (postwar section) and five or six residential complexes surrounding the city. We took the Intourist general tour and saw parks, city buildings, and the house where the Russian writer Pushkin lived while he was in exile in 1823 and 1824. There were no old castles, palaces, or churches in Kishinev, since it had suffered heavily during several wars. What had been there in previous times did not survive. Our guide treated us to the usual historical review of the area:

"Kishinev was first mentioned in a letter written by a Moldavian prince, Alexander the Good, in 1420. This sun-kissed land with black fertile soil on the banks of the Byd River fell under Turkish control and for most of the next four hundred years remained so. The town was destroyed by the Tatars about the end of the seventeenth century, but rose again at the beginning of the eighteenth century, mainly through the efforts of the Armenians who settled in the region and developed its trade. In 1712, Prince Mavokordat ceded Kishinev to the Good Friday Monastery, and from that point the town entered a new period of prosperity. Its trade and crafts expanded, even though the Turkish yoke and oppressive feudal organization hampered the city's economic life. Twice during the eighteenth century Kishinev was burned down. A period of rapid growth began after the city was ceded to Russia in 1812 at the end of the Russo-Turkish War. The city's growth was spurred following the completion of the railroad in the 1870s. The first schools were opened in 1873, and by the end of the nineteenth century, there were five secondary schools, three primary schools, and a public library.

"With the reign of Russia's last Czar, Nicholas II (who reigned from 1894 to 1917), religious persecution increased, especially in southern Russia. Sectarian groups who refused to recognize the state religion and perform such state obligations as military service suffered the most. The state, under Nicholas II's direction, confiscated the estates and funds of the Armenian church and harassed the Jews. The Jewish harassment reached a climax in 1903 with an organized massacre of the Jews in and around Kishinev.

"During this period, the worker's movement was particularly active in Kishinev. Its organization centered on the clandestine print shop from which Lenin's newspaper *Iskra* was issued. This press was destroyed by the czar's police in 1902, and violent demonstrations erupted in 1905, with many persons killed.

"Following the revolution, Kishinev was transferred to Rumania, in 1918, under the name of Chisinau. The city remained under Rumanian control until June 1940, when it was again united with the USSR. One year later, in June 1941, Hitler's Nazis overran the area and occupied the city until August 1944. Two-thirds of the city was devastated by the Nazis before they withdrew. Once again, the city rebuilt to take its place as the modern capital of the Moldavian Soviet Socialist Republic."

Gloria and I stayed at the Intourist Hotel in Kishinev. We hadn't been in our room more than ten minutes when there was a knock at the door. When I opened it, a middle-aged gentleman greeted us in rapid Russian.

"*Nye ponimayu* [I don't understand]," I told him as he rattled off an explanation of why he was at the door.

"*Deutsch?*"

"*Nyet. Angliiskii.*"

At that point he gave up on the language and got down to business. He produced a package and carefully unwrapped it. It contained a cut crystal dish, probably antique. He tried to hand it to me for inspection.

"*Nyet*," I said, refusing to take the dish.

Undaunted, he went on with his sales pitch. I cut him off with "*Nyet spasibo* [No, thank you]," and closed the door. It's illegal to export antiques, heirlooms, or art objects without a special permit. I wasn't about to buy any family keepsakes or heirlooms in the hallway of the hotel.

In the various cities we visited, the guides had pointed marriage palaces out to us. In Kishinev, we got the opportunity to visit one. The marriage palace in this city had formerly been the residence of a wealthy landowner. For a couple to get married in the Soviet Union, they must go to the marriage palace and register their intent. There is a three-month waiting period to avoid sudden decisions. Marriages take place on Fridays and Saturdays, while Wednesdays are set aside for divorces. (It is much easier to get a divorce than it is to get married. The marriage is dissolved without a waiting period.)

To be married, the couple return to the marriage palace after the three-month waiting period. The groom is dressed in a dark suit while the bride may wear a long, white wedding gown or a short white dress. Usually the couple arrive by taxi, which is decked out with wedding bells or giant golden rings on top and crepe paper streamers on the hood. On several occasions, we saw a bride doll in complete wedding dress tied to the front of the car. The doll signifies the couple's wish for a baby girl; a teddy bear is used if they wish for a baby boy. After the ceremony, the couple will go to a war memorial and place flowers on the grave site of the unknown soldier, then to the wedding party, where there is plenty of vodka, champagne, and dancing.

Chapter 15
Odessa: Wednesday, Yesterday, or Tomorrow, but Not Today

We continued our drive to the Black Sea, heading for Odessa, slowly and carefully, since we already had one traffic warning on our tourist card. The country was hilly for the first hundred miles from Kishinev, with vineyards and orchards. As we got near Odessa, the land flattened and we saw wheat fields and more orchards. We entered the western edge of Odessa and, after a quick tour of the city, located the Black Sea Hotel. I went to the Intourist Service Bureau and found things in the usual state of confusion.

"We received your itinerary a few weeks ago and expected you here on Wednesday, according to that itinerary. Last week we received a telegram from Chernovtsy changing your arrival to yesterday. Last night we got a telegram from Kishinev saying you would arrive tomorrow. And here you are today!"

"Yes," I agreed. "There does seem to be some confusion. But we are here today and would like to stay one night."

The Intourist agent shook her head slowly as she went to check with the hotel reservation clerk. They went round and round about Wednesday, yesterday, tomorrow, and today. Finally, the Intourist agent won, and we were given a room and a key card. We retired to our room for a short nap and a chance to read up on the local history before we started to explore the "Pearl of the Black Sea."

The tour book explained that the coast of the Black Sea has been dotted with Greek settlements for 3,000 years. Following the Greeks, the Slavs and then the Turks occupied the area around Odessa. The Turkish garrison of Hadji Bey had successfully defended the area against the Poles. In 1789, a detachment of Russian soldiers and Cossacks, under the command of General Suvorov, took the fortress by assault. Suvorov was directed by Catherine the Great to rebuild the fortress and build a naval port. A Frenchman, the Duc de Richelieu, who was appointed as the first governor of Odessa, had the city laid out with spacious squares and broad, tree-lined avenues. It had the well-designed appearance of a French town of that period.

From 1814 to 1849, Odessa had the status of a free port open to the Western world. The town's population grew with a mixture of Russians, Ukrainians, Greeks, Bulgarians, Armenians, Turks, Jews, Moldavians, Italians, and Gypsies. In 1854, during the Crimean War, Odessa was bombarded by an Anglo-French squadron. The British man-of-war, HMS *Tiger*, ran ashore during the battle, and a gun from that ship now stands in front of the city's palace, overlooking the bay. The British and French ships were finally driven off by the four cannons of the fort.

Odessa remained a cosmopolitan city with a large foreign population during the second half of the nineteenth century and became active in the revolutionary movement. During the 1905 revolution, mutiny on board the cruiser *Potemkin* was savagely suppressed by the czar's troops, focusing attention on the city. Twelve years later, in 1917, the Bolshiviks made a strong bid for power, but this was successfully put down by the White Russians with aid from the Austro-Germans, French, and British. The Bolsheviks finally took control of Odessa in 1920.

During the Second World War, Odessa was one of the first towns to be bombarded and invaded by the Nazis. After a three-month siege, the town was occupied, largely by Rumanian soldiers. After three years of occupation, the Nazi and Rumanian armies withdrew.

After our nap, we walked along the seaside promenade that overlooks the harbor and found statues of Pushkin, palaces, museums, and coffee shops. In this resort seaport of 1 million people, most of the important buildings and historic sights are built along the bluff that commands the west side of the harbor. Toward the northern end of the promenade, we encountered the famous Potemkin Steps. These steps, numbering over a hundred, lead down to the harbor and were originally intended to be the main entrance to the city. They have been used in several Russian movies, including *Potemkin*, where czarist soldiers massacred the townspeople as they came down the steps.

Today the scene from the steps is breathtaking rather than gruesome, with the extensive port facilities lying in a panaroma below. We saw thirty or forty vessels in port being serviced. Outside the breakwater, another forty or fifty ships setting at anchor waiting their turn could be counted. An escalator has been built alongside the famous steps so now it is possible to walk down the steps and ride back up for five kopeks.

Not far from the top of the steps is the Odessa opera house. The original wooden building, constructed in the early 1800s, faced the harbor. That building burned in 1873, and the current stone opera house was built in 1880 with the entrance facing the city rather than the harbor. Whether you are an opera fan or not, you must visit the opera house in Odessa. It is said to rival the Vienna opera house and to be one of the most beautiful in the world. It certainly was the most beautiful one Gloria and I have ever seen. During the Nazi occupation of World War II, there was some damage, but the opera house was operating again by 1946. In 1967, it underwent a major renovation, with over fifteen pounds of

After the original wooden opera house burned down, the new stone Odessa opera house was built in 1880.

gold used on the gilding alone.

The Opera house is a roundish building made of a gray-brown stone. Inside the main entrance, at the front of the building, was a staircase that could have come straight off of a Hollywood movie set. The golden marble stairs were adorned by exquisite brass statues. It's the custom for ladies to be photographed descending the three-story–high staircase. Young ladies line up on the second level in front of the gigantic fifteen-foot mirror to fix their hair, straighten their dress, and do their last-minute primping before they glide down the magnificent staircase.

The opera house is a roundish building made of a gray-in the four balconies, and in the thirty-two boxes that line the gilded horseshoe-shaped auditorium. The ceiling is decorated with frescoes depicting scenes from Shakespeare's plays, and the entire setting is crowned with a huge crystal chandelier.

We were able to get box seats to see *Eugene Onegin*, an opera written by Tchaikovsky, based upon a story by Pushkin. It was very exciting to see an opera written by a Russian performed in Russian. The setting was early–nineteenth-century Russia, and the costumes were beautiful, well made, and authentic. The cost of the box seats, located near the stage, was four dollars. The entire setting was breathtaking, and it was well worth the price of admission.

Early the next morning, I jogged down to the Black Sea, about a mile from our hotel. Since the weather was cool, I debated whether or not to try the water. I was encouraged by the thirty or forty people exercising vigorously on the beach and splashing around in the water. So I took off my sweatshirt and plunged in. The cold water was a shock.

It's not salty! was my first thought. I had always imagined the Black Sea as being warm and salty. Wrong on both counts. I paddled around in the water for ten or fifteen minutes, playing in the two-foot–high waves, then got out, took a shower, and ran back to the hotel.

Gloria and I decided to check with Intourist about a tour of the catacombs under Odessa.

"You must have a group of fifteen or more," said the prim, blond Intourist representative.

"May we go and just look around them by ourselves?"

"Impossible! Tourists get lost in the catacombs."

The catacombs are limestones caves that run for 200 miles under the city of Odessa. They have been used by revolutionaries and criminals for hundreds of years to hide from those in power. During World War II, when the Nazis occupied Odessa for three years, the Resistance used the catacombs as their headquarters. The Nazis dynamited them, flooded them, and used poisonous gas to force the people out, without success. The Resistance had their barracks, training rooms, baths, fresh-water wells, and bakeries in the catacombs. We were disappointed in not being able to tour them, but decided that we would come back to Odessa sometime in the future to accomplish this.

For breakfast, we tried some delicious *bliny* covered with *smetana* (sour cream). Bliny are also served with jelly, meat, or caviar.

Chapter 16
Return to Kiev: Supper with TASS

After a morning walk down to the beach for our farewell to the Black Sea, Gloria and I started on the eight-hour drive to Kiev. Flat land covered with orchards gave way to rolling wheat fields about 100 miles north of Odessa. From the top of the hills, it was possible to see wheat fields stretching for miles in all directions.

Ever since we had entered the Soviet Union, we had noticed charming young girls dressed in black uniforms with pretty white aprons trimmed with lace. "They are schoolgirls," an Intourist guide had said. "It is examination time and that is the uniform they wear for special occasions. Usually they wear black aprons, but for special times the aprons are white."

I now decided that I must have a photo of these young ladies in their pretty uniforms. I saw a group of four girls at a rural bus stop and stopped to talk with them.

"Hello. I'm an American tourist and would like to take your picture in your beautiful dresses," I said in Russian. "May I take your photograph?"

The four girls in their early teens looked at each other and giggled.

"*Nyet*," said the pretty blond who appeared to be the oldest of the four.

"Please," I pleaded.

"You give us photo?" asked the curly-hair brunette closest to me.

"Yes. I have a special camera that gives you a picture

The Soviet schoolgirls wear black school uniforms with white pinafores, during holidays or examination periods.

right away." Gloria and I had purchased a Polaroid camera especially for the trip as a conversation starter and so we could use photos as trading material.

Two of the girls agreed to the photo and got up to comb their hair and pose. They checked their aprons and posed arm in arm for the photo. I took a couple of pictures and gave them to the girls as they were developing. After seeing the magic of Polaroid, the third girl decided she wanted her picture taken. I took one of her alone and one of the three girls together.

The temptation was too much for the blond girl who had been so negative at the outset. "*Vse* [all]," she said.

The four of them lined up. I took four Polaroids one for each of them. As I handed the last picture to the curly-haired brunette, she took a blue bow and bell that was pinned to her apron and pinned it to my shirt.

"*Dlya vas* [For you]," she said.

The girls marveled at their photos.

"Do any of you speak English?" I asked.

"*Nyet*," they replied.

None of them was brave enough to try an English conversation. As I went to the car, they wished us a safe journey and waved as we drove away.

We had carried a quart of oil for the car into the Soviet Union with us from Finland. During the past two weeks, we had traveled 5,000 kilometers and I had used the oil and needed to get some more. I checked with Intourist and obtained some vouchers for eighteen kopeks each good for a quarter-liter of oil. At the first benzine station stop of the day, I got my gas and then went back to talk to the lady at the office window about the oil.

"*Nyet masla*," she said and slammed the window closed. The conversation was over.

As I walked away, one of the other customers came over and asked me to come with him. He took me around behind the benzine station to a small garage that served as a service and repair station. He pointed to one of the three doors. "*Maslo*," he said.

I knocked and a mechanic opened the door. I handed him my oil vouchers. "*Maslo?*" I asked.

He shook his head yes. *"Nyet vouchers,"* he said. *"Dengi."* He rubbed his fingers together as the international sign for money.

I pulled out some rubles while he went inside and came back with a two-and-a-half–liter can of oil.

"Nyet," I said. *"Odin* [one] liter."

"Nyet," he said, handing me the entire can.

I paid him three rubles and took the oil to the car. I only needed a little oil, but decided to take what I could get. The two and a half liters was enough for a complete oil change for the Opel Kadett.

We returned to the Lybed Hotel in Kiev. There I went to see Intourist about changing our itinerary.

"Mr. Johnson! You are back!" said the head of Intourist as if she had never expected to see us again.

"Yes. Can you check with Rovno and Uzhgorod to see if it is okay to change our itinerary as we previously discussed?"

"It is not necessary. You come tomorrow and tell me what time you are leaving for Rovno and I will send a telegram. In Rovno, you will discuss Uzhgorod. Only there can you make the change."

"Okay. One day at a time."

As I considered the perennial question "Where shall we eat tonight?" Gloria had a suggestion: "The hotel restaurant has *shashlyk* on the menu."

"What is *shashlyk?*"

"It's a Georgian shish kebab with pieces of fat stuck between each piece of meat. The meat comes out really tender and juicy," she said.

Such a treat I couldn't refuse. As had been common throughout our trip, the waitress seated us at a partially occupied table. In this case, it was occupied by a middle-aged blond man in a blue leisure suit.

"Zdravstvuite," he said as we sat down.

"*Zdravstvuite*," we replied.

We ordered supper and attempted to get a clue to our dinner companion's nationality. We had shared tables with Austrians, Germans, Rumanians, and a few Russians.

After a few minutes and some conversation between Gloria and me, our supper companion asked, "What part of the Midwest are you from?" in perfect English.

"Dayton, Ohio."

"I knew you were from the Midwest by your accent. I am a TASS correspondent specializing in languages."

We had a delightful discussion about the Soviet Union, world news (with which Gloria and I had been out of touch with for three weeks), and the U.S.A. We found this custom of seating people together to fill up tables, while obviously intended to make more efficient use of dining space available, had a delightful side benefit. We met some interesting people in that fashion. That was the main objective of our trip—to meet and talk with Russian people. Before we finished our meal, our dinner companion downed his last glass of vodka and excused himself.

"I have to catch the nine o'clock train for Moscow," he said. "I must take a box of candy for my son. He wanted to come with me on this trip, but he couldn't because of examinations in school. The candy is a reward for his patience."

As we ate our delicious *shashlyk*, the band came in and started reconstructing the sound system. They carried amplifiers, speakers, and electronic mixers down from the second-floor ballroom. During our previous stay here, they spent the entire supper hour dismantling the sound system and hauling it upstairs. We had seen a lot of the band in the two nights, but never did hear them play any music. After supper, Gloria and I walked around the area surrounding the hotel and found an antique shop.

"Look at those beautiful copper samovars in the window,"

Gloria said. "Think I could carry one of those home on the airplane?"

Before I could answer, a Russian lady sharing the window with us interrupted. "My folks had a samovar exactly like those when I grew up. I have a small electric one now. Can't afford to use a real one anymore," she mused in Russian.

"Neither can we," I told Gloria firmly.

Chapter 17
Rovno: The Strawberry Lady

With road construction in Kiev, Gloria and I had a little problem finding our way out of town. After a short tour of the suburbs, we got started to Rovno, situated in western Ukraine, 200 miles west of Kiev. The landscape was flat along the route, with some low hills. The crops consisted mainly of wheat with an occasional field of corn. We passed through small rural villages every fifteen or twenty miles.

About an hour out of Kiev, we entered the village of Brusilov. I don't want to give the impression that Brusilov is a small town, but they didn't have enough traffic to warrant a crossroad. In the middle of the town was a one-lane dirt road going off to the left. The one-story tile and stucco houses were scattered one deep along each side of the road. A faded green fence gave the residences a hint of privacy. Near the middle of the village, we spied pails of fresh strawberries sitting alongside the road on stools or makeshift tables. The ladies who owned the strawberries were sitting back by the fence or up on the front porch of their houses waiting for a buyer.

"We can't pass up an opportunity to get some fresh strawberries," I told Gloria as I drove over to the side of the road. A plump middle-aged lady was off her porch and out to meet me before I got to her strawberry stand. As I approached, she started her sales pitch, expounding on how big, sweet, and juicy her strawberries were.

"How much?" I asked in Russian.

She wasn't finished with the sales pitch yet and continued to tell me how fresh they were, how plump, how firm.

139

"How much?" I repeated.

"*Dva rublya* [Two rubles]," she said holding up a thumb and an index finger.

"I'll take one pan," I said. As I held out my open plastic bag, she poured strawberries into it. I gave her the two rubles and asked her, "Please, may I take your photograph?"

"Why would you want my photograph?"

"To show my friends in America how beautiful your strawberries are," I said.

"Why not?" she shrugged as she tucked her loose hair back under her multicolored kerchief and straightened her apron.

As I got my Polaroid ready, the neighbor ladies perked up with curiosity. They started drifting over to see what was happening. I took one Polaroid of the woman standing by her basket of strawberries. As I handed her the undeveloped Polaroid, Gloria joined us. The strawberry lady watched with delight as the image started to take shape. Her eyes got as big as saucers.

"*Ochen khorosho* [Very good]," she said to Gloria as the picture of the red strawberries and her blue skirt developed in vivid color. By that time, the neighbor ladies were converging on us.

"*Ochen khorosho*," she repeated, showing the photo to each of her neighbors.

"*Khorosho!*" each repeated in turn with a raise of the eyebrows.

By now, our small crowd was attracting the attention of the passing motorists. Several stopped to see what the gathering was about. Before the strawberry lady would sell them any strawberries, she had to show each one of them her pictures. She was busy showing and selling and selling and showing. Our sizable crowd drew more attention, and cars were now stopping in the middle of the road. The drivers abandoned

140

I bought a pan of home-grown strawberries from a friendly woman in a small Ukrainian village. My Polaroid camera attracted a huge crowd and caused a traffic jam before I left.

their vehicles to get a better view of the goings-on. With all the new additions, we had a frenzy going around the strawberry lady. People were milling around, feeling the strawberries, looking at her photograph, gossiping, and having a good time. Gloria and I decided to go, so we said good-bye and headed for the car.

"Wait!" cried the strawberry lady as she ran after us with another pan of strawberries.

"*Nyet. Nyet,* no more," I said. "We have enough."

"*Da. Da,* you take," she insisted. She poured another pan of strawberries into our bulging bag. We shook hands and made our way back to the car. By the time we drove off, the strawberry lady had sold all her strawberries and was proudly admiring her photograph. The customers were slowly drifting back to their cars, and the neighbors were standing around in little knots, savoring the excitement of the day.

About midday, Gloria and I came to a deserted lake on the edge of a small village. Since the car was muddy again from driving in the rain, we pulled over to wash it. I got out our Soviet bucket (especially purchased for this purpose) and filled it in the lake. Within a few minutes, a GAI car pulled up. The officer came over to check our documents. He took them back to his car, studied them, then returned to us and asked where the car was from.

"Denmark."

"Why not U.S.?" he asked in Russian, noting our U.S. passports.

"Rented in Denmark," I said as I pulled out the rental contract.

"Ah," he replied. Then in the dust on the back of the car he traced the letters "U.S." He joked that those letters turned around were "SU" or "Soviet Union." We laughed at his joke. He wished us a good day and went back to his car. I had not noticed during the conversation, but again our activity by the roadside had attracted attention. Three trucks had pulled over, and the drivers came over to the lake to wash their hands and faces and talk with the GAI officer. A motorcycle came by and stopped, as did a tractor and another car. Everyone stood chatting for a while and then left. It doesn't take much to attract a crowd.

By midafternoon, Gloria and I arrived at Rovno, a beautiful city of 150,000 people located in the middle of the Ukrainian wheat belt. We checked in at the Mir [Peace] Hotel and spoke with the Intourist agent.

"Will you send a telegram to Uzhgorod when we leave tomorrow?"

"Not necessary. You already have reservations."

"We did have," I explained, showing him my original itinerary. "But I'm not so sure anymore, since Moscow sent this telegram."

I showed him the telegram changing our itinerary.

"If you would like, I will send a telegram and ask if you still have reservations. You come back tomorrow at nine o'clock and see if we have a reply by then," he said.

We probably should have kept quiet and assumed we had reservations in Uzhgorod, but we didn't understand exactly how the system operated and didn't want to get crossways with the authorities. We would wait for the telegram. We picked up a couple of the Intourist pamphlets, and while we were looking through them, the Intourist representative gave us a short historical sketch of Rovno:

"The town was founded in the thirteenth century under Polish rule. It was here that Prince Alexis the Black of Volhynia defeated the Lithuanian army in 1282. From the fifteenth to the seventeenth centuries, the town belonged to the Ostrovski family, who built a strong, fortified castle. During the eighteenth century, the castle was altered to rococo style by the Polish magnate Lubomirski.

"With the partition of Poland in 1795, Rovno fell to Russia and became the chief town of the district. There were also Czech settlers in the surrounding area and many Jewish craftsmen in the town itself. Rovno returned to the newly reestablished state of Poland in 1918, but twenty-one years later, in 1939, was annexed by the Soviet Union and incorporated into the Ukraine. In 1941, Rovno was the center of a fierce struggle by partisans against the Nazis. It was occupied until 1945."

On Sunday afternoon, Gloria and I walked through one of the many beautiful parks in town. Since it was Sunday, the park was filled with the townspeople. The little girls were dressed in knitted dresses, fancy little hair bows, and new shoes. This was their day to be taken to the park to play. Like most of the Soviet parks, this one was loaded with fountains and running water. One fountain had a six-foot–high Saint George fighting a twenty-foot–long dragon. Water gushed out of the dragon's mouth and nostrils, filling up the large basin surrounding the statue. The edge of the fountain was ringed with children getting their pictures taken or splashing in the water. We didn't see or hear any parents chasing them or yelling, "Don't play in the water! You'll get your good clothes wet." The parents seemed to feel that the children were there to play and that a little water wouldn't hurt them.

In the corner of the park was a driving area set up for bicycles. The sidewalk had a center stripe and was like a regular highway, with stoplights, rotaries, and all the regular highway signs. Children on bicycles rode over the route, observing all the signals and pedestrian walkways. It was a good way to start driver's education and also to make a little fun for the children.

Rovno was of special interest to us, since our tutor, Mrs. Chazin, was from this area. "Be sure to pay special attention to the old churches and the countryside around Rovno," she had told us, "so you can describe them in detail when you come home." Her family had left the area during the turmoil preceding the First World War. Gloria and I walked around the older parts of the city and took lots of photographs of the churches, buildings, and houses we thought would have been there in the early 1900s. (These photos were later confiscated during a misunderstanding at the Russian border.)

For supper, we ordered a Ukrainian dish of meat with mushroom sauce similar to beef Stroganoff. The hostess seated us with a couple from Heidelberg, Germany. They were camping through the Soviet Union.

"Camping in Russia not good," the husband told us in a combination of German and English.

"You speak Russian?" I asked.

"*Nein,*" he shrugged.

"How is the road to the Soviet border?" I asked.

"Ah. Very rough and very hilly. You go slow," he continued.

"Yes. We've already encountered that kind of road in the Soviet Union."

After some wine, dessert and coffee, the waitress brought the checks. The German fellow looked at his bill and let out a low whistle.

"Ah," he moaned. "I don't think I have enough Russian money."

When the waitress came back, he showed her that he only had a few rubles. To dramatize it, he held his billfold upside down and shook it. Nothing came out. He then looked at us, laughed, and crossed his wrists to signify "jail." The waitress called the Intourist agent over, and after some negotiations, our German friend was able to cash more marks into rubles and avoid jail.

Chapter 18
Uzhgorod:
"Why Did You Change Your Itinerary?"

It was pouring down rain as we drove from Rovno to the border town of Uzhgorod. The country outside Rovno was flat for the first hundred miles; then it changed to low, rolling hills. We came upon a field where vines were growing up the telephone poles. It turned out to be an area where they grow hops for the beer industry. The telephone poles were used to support the long, horizontal wires, and the hops grow up the vertical wires like beans, stretching fifteen or twenty feet in the air.

During our trip through the Soviet Union, Gloria and I had noticed that there were no castles, like those that are so prominent in Spain, Germany, and England. In their early history, the Russians traded with and traveled through the Middle East countries rather than Europe. The fortresses that were built in those early days were the kremlins, or citadels, along the banks of the rivers, designed to protect the villages. However, in a little town outside of Lvov, we saw a castle, or a vast country estate, on a hilltop. We turned off the main road and drove through the small village to get a better view of the eighteenth-century complex. The buildings and grounds around it were well kept, indicating that it must now be used as a museum or school.

We continued the trip to the area of Skola, where hills changed abruptly to mountains, similar to those of western

146

Virginia or Pennsylvania. The houses also changed from stone to wood, due to the abundance of timber in the area. Four or five thousand feet above the flatlands, there were some picturesque mountain villages reminiscent of Austria. Neat wooden houses with small brightly painted barns lined the roadside. Huge piles of firewood were stacked against the barn. The small logs were each cut to exactly the same length, as though by machine, and stacked neatly as bricks. A freshly cut tree branch was attached to each side of the house, satisfying some local custom. At suppertime, we arrived at Uzhgorod, about ten miles from the Hungarian border. The first thing I did was find the hotel and check in with Intourist.

"Ah, Mr. Johnson. We are so glad to see you," said the Intourist agent as I handed her our documents. "You have caused us quite a bit of trouble changing your itinerary back and forth," she continued. "In the future it would be better for you to firm up your plans before you submit the itinerary."

"Me? Firm up our plans! I didn't change our itinerary. Moscow did."

"Why would they do that?"

"I was hoping you could tell me."

"No. When we received the telegram from Moscow canceling your stay, we assumed you had departed from the Soviet Union."

"Are we all set with a room here tonight?"

"Of course. Here is your key card. You can get your key at the desk. Have a pleasant stay in Uzhgorod."

When I went back to the car to get Gloria and the luggage, I found she was being held hostage by a Soviet youth.

"He was asking all about the car," she said as I walked up. "How much does it cost, how fast does it go, how many horsepower?"

"*Ochen khorosho* [Very good]," said the teenage boy as he patted the car.

147

I talked with him for a while about the car; then he got down to business.

"Cigarettes?" he asked.

"*Nyet.* I don't have any cigarettes," I said.

"You sell jeans? I pay twenty rubles," he offered.

"No jeans."

"Thirty rubles," he said.

"No jeans. I have no jeans to sell," I said.

"You sell shirt?" he asked, feeling my yellow Van Heusen shirt.

"No, I don't want to sell anything," I replied.

"Maybe she will sell something," he said, turning to Gloria.

"No. She doesn't want to sell anything," I insisted.

The young man finally got discouraged and trotted off to hassle another carload of tourists that had just pulled up to the hotel.

"I wonder how much he'd give me for that yellow-and-black blouse that I never liked?" mused Gloria as we carried our luggage into the hotel.

After dropping our luggage in our room, I settled down with the Intourist guide to bone up on the local history:

> Uzhgorod, which was founded in the 8th century, is one of the oldest Slavic towns. It was originally the chief town of the White Croat tribe. In the 12th century it belonged to Kievan Russia and was the site of a 13th century castle. The area next fell under the yoke of the Mogyars, the nomadic hordes that settled the area around Hungary. In the 18th century the Austrians took possession and controlled Uzhgorod until 1919, when the Austro-Hungarian Empire was broken up and the city passed to Czechoslovakia. Following the Second World War the city became part of the Ukraine.

Rested up from our drive, Gloria and I decided to take a walk along the river through the old part of town, which has been turned into a huge pedestrian shopping mall. The area covered ten or fifteen blocks and was filled with old, narrow, brick streets, squares, and hundreds of shops. Many foreigners cross the border to buy vodka and souvenirs. Often they don't travel any farther into the Soviet Union than Uzhgorod.

Gloria and I returned to our hotel for supper. As we went into the restaurant, we were met by a maitre d' who looked like Jonathan Winters.

"*Obed* [Supper]?" he asked.

"*Da*."

"You pay American?" he asked expectantly.

"No. We pay rubles," I replied.

"Oh," he said with a sad note in his voice.

The supper was fantastic, complete with wine, salad, meat, potatoes, dessert, and coffee. The total cost was five dollars per person. We listened to Ukrainian folk music furnished by a loud Ukrainian band until 11:00 P.M.

Chapter 19
Chop Crossing:
Telephone Poles Are Restricted

Gloria and I woke early, with the sun streaming in our room announcing the start of another beautiful day. For our last day in the Soviet Union, we had a substantial breakfast of pancakes, cheese, and eggs at the buffet and headed for the border. After a short, scenic drive, we arrived at the Chop Immigration and Customs checkpoint around 10:30 A.M.

The customs guard directed us up the ramp to the second level of the customs building. The customs official greeted us courteously and invited us to park and come inside to fill out the currency declaration. Gloria and I entered the large waiting room and sat down at a table in the middle to fill out the declaration. A coffee bar was at one end of the room and a TV with a dozen chairs at the other end. The only people in the room were four or five guards and a couple of civilians watching TV. After completing our currency forms, we decided to have a cup of coffee.

"Can I have one of those big chocolate bars?" asked Gloria.

"No. I've only enough rubles for coffee, and I want to take one of them home as a souvenir."

At that time, a man in his thirties came up to us and introduced himself.

"My name is Peter," he said with a heavy British accent. "I work for Intourist. How was your visit to the Soviet Union?"

"We really enjoyed it," said Gloria.

"Have you spent all your rubles?" he asked.

"Yes," I said. "All except this one-ruble note, which I

plan to take home as a souvenir."

"That is not allowed," he said.

"I can't take one ruble out?"

"No. Not even one. You must spend it."

"Oh, boy!" said Gloria. "We'll take that big chocolate bar right there."

The customs official came in and said something to Peter.

"He'd like you to move your car up to the inspection point now," he told us. "Let's get cracking."

We pulled the car forward over an inspection pit. Three Soviet officials searched the car thoroughly, checking for secret compartments and stuff hidden in the gas tank or inside the doors. Two other officials went through our luggage with a fine-tooth comb. They opened every package, checked in our shoes, and felt the lining of the suitcases for contraband.

The chief of immigrations checked Gloria's purse and my briefcase. He commented that I had a lot of papers in my briefcase and he would have to take it inside for closer examination.

"You can put the rest of your luggage back in the car," Peter told us.

We visited with Peter and Marsha, another Intourist agent, after the chief left.

"I'm interested in what you thought of the Soviet people," confided Marsha.

"They have all been very kind and courteous to us," I said. "Anytime we've gotten lost or needed help, the people have gone out of their way to help."

"I love the Soviet children and the cats," added Gloria.

"I wonder what's taking so long?" I asked Peter.

"Oh, I'm sure it's nothing. They'll be back in a few minutes and you can be on your way."

Sure enough, in a few moments the chief of immigrations came back.

"Would you please move your car off the inspection pit

151

and park it on the first level?" asked the chief.

"Park it where?" I asked.

"I'll ride with you and show you," the chief said.

He guided me off the ramp and to a parking area directly under the ramp.

"Would you please wait in this room?" asked the chief, pointing to a door with bars across the window.

"Will it be long?" I asked.

"No, I don't think so," said the chief.

Gloria and I went into the small waiting room. There was a round table in the middle of the room with four chairs around it. Other than that, the room was bare. There was a door going off to the toilets, one going to some offices, and one window with bars overlooking the bridge to Hungary.

"Why do you suppose they asked us to wait here?" asked Gloria.

"Probably just routine," I answered halfheartedly.

We sat down and waited about thirty minutes. Finally the chief of immigrations returned with the two Intourist agents.

"How many pictures did you take in the Soviet Union?" asked the chief.

"Oh, about six or seven hundred," I answered.

"Why did you take so many pictures?" he asked.

"I always take a lot of pictures when I travel. We like to look at pictures of the places we visited."

"You know there are restrictions on what you can photograph in the Soviet Union," the chief reminded me.

"Yes. I understand the photographic restrictions, and I observed them," I assured him.

"I would like to develop one roll of your film just to be sure," replied the chief.

"These rolls are Kodachrome and your Intourist guidebook states that you do not have the proper developing equipment for Kodachrome in the Soviet Union."

"Oh, the guidebook is out of date. We have such a process and the proper equipment," the chief assured me. "Do I have your permission to develop a roll?"

"No," I said. "These slides are important to me, and I would rather you would not develop them and ruin the color."

"I am going to develop a roll of your film before you leave the country," insisted the chief.

"I think you'd better let him have a roll if we ever want to get out of here," whispered Gloria.

"Well, in that case, of course I'll give you permission to develop my film," I conceded.

I laid out the seventeen rolls of film on the table, and the chief selected one at random and asked me to sign it. I signed the can of film and set it back on the table, off to the side of the other film. At that point, a customs official came out of the door to the office and told the chief he had a phone call. The chief and both Intourist agents went into the office and left Gloria and me to ourselves. I sat eyeing the film. I had the feeling we were being watched, and I hoped Gloria wouldn't touch the film. They might be testing us to see if we would try to substitute another can for the one that the chief had selected.

"Would you get my knitting out of the car?" asked Gloria.

"Sure," I said and went out and brought her knitting bag back in.

Gloria and I sat for two hours, waiting for the chief to come back. Gloria knitted and I spent the time dozing or looking longingly out the window at the Hungarian border. Finally the chief returned, along with Peter and Marsha.

"I'll get this roll of film developed," he announced leaving the room with the roll of film I had signed.

Gloria and I talked with Peter and Marsha about the weather, the Soviet school system, and travel. In about an hour, the chief returned with a troubled look on his face.

"You understand that there are restrictions on what you may photograph in the Soviet Union?" asked the chief of immigrations.

"Yes, I understand. We are not to photograph military installations, airports, railroad bridges, or subjects that might be considered degrading."

"These slides violate our photographic restrictions."

"Which slides?"

"This one," he said pointing to my roll of color slides, which were now black and white. "It is our military communications system."

"That's a picture of a field of wheat," I said.

"Ah! But there is a telephone pole in the corner of the photograph. Military communications."

"A telephone pole is restricted?"

"Yes. And this photograph is a panoramic view of a river port."

"Yes, that's a shot of Kiev from the park."

"Also restricted. No panoramic views allowed."

"But that's the same view that is on the postcard I bought at the hotel."

"Doesn't matter. No panoramic photographs allowed."

He pointed to another slide and continued. "This is a photograph of a strategic road crossing of military value and also restricted."

"That is the road near Suzdal. There was a one-lane dirt road going off to the side. I took a photograph to show people that the road sign is in your Cyrillic alphabet, not in Roman characters," I said.

"These photographs are restricted. I will have to develop all your film," he insisted.

"But you're ruining it," I argued. "The roll you developed is black and white and all streaked."

"No matter. I must develop it all," he said as he scooped up the rest of the film and left.

"Bad business," Peter consoled us. "We have many silly restrictions in this country."

Marsha tried to cheer us up by telling about her five-year-old son and the cute things he was doing. Somehow it didn't help much.

About fifteen minutes later, the chief came back with the travel diary I had been keeping on the trip.

"Why did you write so much about the Soviet Union?" he asked.

"I keep notes on the places we visit, what we saw, and what I took pictures of," I explained.

"What will you do with these notes?"

"When we get home, I'll use them to give lectures about our trip."

"Who will you give these lectures to?"

"To our friends, the Russian Club at the university, and maybe professional clubs in our city."

"Do they pay you to give these lectures?"

"No. I don't get paid."

"Why would you spend all this money to come over here and then go home and give free lectures?"

"I know it sounds dumb, but it's fun to share a trip with other people, even if they don't pay for it."

"Strange," he said, shaking his head like he wasn't convinced of the purpose of our trip.

At that point, our discussion took a new turn. He produced Gloria's pocket calendar and asked us to explain the rows of stars alongside the names of the cities we had visited.

"That's my cat count," said Gloria, laying her knitting aside.

"Your what?" asked Peter, not willing to trust his ears.

"My cat count. I count cats while Allen drives. I mark

155

the number of cats I see along the way on the calendar. One star represents two cats."

"Would you like to tell the chief of immigrations that these cryptic marks on the calendar are cats?" said Peter.

"Why do you count cats?" asked the chief.

"I like cats. I watch for them along the road and keep count of them to pass the time."

"You mean like bird-watching?" said Peter.

"Yes. Some people watch for birds. I watch for cats."

"In other words, you are a 'catologist,' " mused Peter.

"Yes. I guess you could call it that," replied Gloria, not sure if that was a compliment or a dig.

"Do you believe that cats are used for purposes of black magic?" asked the chief of immigrations.

"Ridiculous. Cats are cats. I like them, and I like to count them. It gives me something to do while Allen is driving."

"What animal do you equate in intelligence to the cat?"

"A dog. Maybe they're not quite as smart and you can dominate them, but some people really like to have them as pets. I like dogs, too, but not well enough to count them on trips."

The chief of immigrations apparently had his cryptology staff trying to decipher the code to relate the number of stars by each city on the calendar to the number of military installations, airports, or something else of importance, but not to the number of cats. He felt that was a farfetched explanation. However, after another hour of conversation and questioning about cats, he decided to drop that line of interrogation.

The chief gathered up my diary and Gloria's cat calendar and left.

"At this point, I don't think the chief feels you intended any malice," said Peter.

"Do you think he will give us back our film and notes?" I asked.

"No. I believe he intends to keep all your film and all your notes."

"Oh." I grunted with a sinking feeling. All my notes and 700 slides down the drain! "Why us?" I asked Peter. "We haven't done anything wrong. We're just here for a friendly visit."

"Yes, I know," said Peter. "Bad business."

At that point, we had spent eight hours at the Chop checkpoint, and it looked as if it might be another eight before we learned our fate. The sun was about to set, and I wondered where we'd be for the next sunrise.

The chief of immigrations finally returned with the rolls of film he had developed.

"We have developed seven rolls of your film and have not found any more forbidden pictures. In a little while, I will permit you to leave, but first you must sign a confession that you took those forbidden photographs," he said.

"Are you going to let us take the photos?" I asked.

"No. The photographs and the notes must remain," he insisted.

The chief then dictated a confession, and I copied it in my own words. I added that I did not believe any of those photographs to be forbidden when I took them. He had me promise to refrain from taking similar photographs if I returned to the Soviet Union. I completed the confession and signed it.

"May we go now?" asked Gloria while she continued to knit.

"No. You wait," said the chief as he left the room.

A few minutes later, he returned carrying ten cans of my film (keeping the other seven). He announced, "I am going to close my eyes to this part of your film. You may take it."

"And my notes?" I asked anxiously.

"Yes. You may take your diary," he said.

"What will you do with the 250 slides you are keeping?"

157

"I will add them to my private collection," he remarked with a smile.

We gathered up the remainder of our film, the notes, and Gloria's knitting and cat calendar and headed for the car. As we placed our belongings in the car, the chief, Peter, and Marsha came out to see us off. Marsha saw my Polaroid camera and asked if I would take a picture of her.

"It is forbidden to take pictures near the border," I replied.

"Oh, go ahead," insisted the chief.

So I took a picture of Marsha and Gloria standing with Peter and the chief of immigrations. As I gave it to Marsha, she gave me a hug and thanked us for the photo.

The chief of immigrations explained that he had only been doing his job and suggested, "Maybe when your grandson comes to visit the Soviet Union, there will be no border."

"I hope so," I replied.

Gloria went to say good-bye to Marsha and gave her the lacy scarf she had knitted during our nine-and-a-half–hour stay.

"*Do svidaniya*," we called to the three of them as we drove off.

The guard at the border stopped us and went into his guard house to call back to the checkpoint. After a two-minute wait, he hung up and raised the gate.

"*Do svidaniya*," he called as we sped across the bridge into Hungary.

As the sun set on our "impossible" Soviet vacation, we crossed the border into Hungary and drove to Budapest.

Chapter 20
Budapest: Culture Shock

At 2:00 A.M., Gloria and I finally reached the Thermal Hotel in Budapest. Hungary turned out to be a culture shock after three weeks in the Soviet Union. The Thermal Hotel was as modern a hotel as we've ever stayed in.

"There's a fridge in our room, and it's stocked with Coca Cola, V-8 juice, beer, chocolates, and peanuts," cried Gloria as I brought the luggage in.

For breakfast, we had fresh fruit, milk, scrambled eggs, sweet rolls, and American-style coffee. It felt almost decadent to eat all that stuff. After breakfast, we toured the city of Budapest. Near the end of the tour, our guide took us to the top of a hill overlooking the river.

"You can get a good panoramic view of Buda on the right side of the river and Pest on the left," she said.

"Is it permissible to take a photograph of the panoramic view?" I asked.

"Why, yes, of course," she said, looking puzzled.

"And the telephone poles?"

"Are you feeling all right?" she asked, a little bewildered by my questions.

"Just wondering."

After the tour, we drove to Vienna, crossing the Hungarian/Austrian border on the way. It took us nine hours to cross the Soviet border, nine minutes to cross the Hungarian border, and nine seconds to cross the Austrian border.

A morning guided tour of Vienna convinced us that we

would have to return for a minimum of a week to really see that city.

In both Austria and Germany, we drove on the Autobahn, or expressway. The speed limit is 130 kilometers an hour, which is faster than I cared to go. It was a nice, smooth, well-marked road with no tractors or lines of trucks. There was a short ferry ride from Puttgarden, Germany, across the Baltic to Rodbyhavn, Denmark.

As we got to Copenhagen, I was somewhat expecting a band or at least a small crowd of well-wishers to welcome us, but we settled for three young folk musicians with a guitar and tambourine.

After a day or two to return our rented magic carpet and visit a few friends in Copenhagen, we caught our Northwest Orient flight to New York. An overnight layover in that city allowed our stomachs to get back on Eastern Daylight Time. The hour-and-a-half flight from New York to Dayton was anticlimactic, but I heaved a sigh of relief as we landed.

"I'll never forget our 'impossible' Russian adventure, but it is always nice to get home," I told Gloria.

"I wonder if Marsha will take good care of that scarf. It was Swedish wool and a Danish pattern," she replied.

Chapter 21
Conclusions

Our "impossible" drive through the Soviet Union convinced me that one on one the people of the world can get along. During our twenty-day stay in the Soviet Union and Hungary, we encountered no animosity. With the exception of the chief of immigration, who was "just doing his job," everyone we met was kind, helpful, and curious to find out what kind of people we were. When we stopped at a benzine station, the locals would flock around the car to inspect the engine, luggage, and inhabitants. If I opened a map, three or four people would crowd around to help me find our way. On the metro, men stood up to give Gloria their seat.

The food in the Soviet Union was not just meat and potatoes, as I had expected. We had some fantastic meals like *shaslik* in Kiev, sturgeon in Moscow, and Stroganoff in Leningrad. The service varied from the best we've had anywhere to mediocre.

We visited many rural villages during our trip and found people living as American farmers did in the 1930s. They have electricity and TV, but no running water. Women still wash clothes in lakes or streams, and a lot of farm work is still done by hand.

The Soviet people have an opportunity to enjoy a variety of cultural programs, from ballet to opera, the circus, and the puppet theater. While the best seats are reserved for foreigners, diplomats, or party officials, there are inexpensive seats available for most performances.

The transportation systems in the Soviet Union are inexpensive, well run, and extensive. The Moscow metro is one of the best in the world and costs only about seven cents a ride. The lack of private cars is compensated for by the grid of bus, train, and metro routes. However, the rural folks must resort to hitchhiking or horse carts to get to the neighboring villages to shop. The over-the-road trucks often stop to pick up three or four people waiting along the road. The rural bus service apparently isn't able to meet the demand of the farmers.

As Gloria and I sat at Pat's farm discussing our trip, the difficulties seemed to become less significant and the pleasures seemed to grow. Would we go back again?

"I can be packed in ten minutes," was Gloria's reply.

Appendix
What Did It Cost?

Several friends asked us "What did the trip cost?" The cost can vary widely, depending on when you travel and how expensive your tastes are. To help estimate the cost of a similar vacation, I'll share our expenses with you.

Some of the first expense were for a U.S. passport ($30), Soviet visa service ($70), traveler's checks ($20), international driver's license ($10), and hotel reservation service fee ($60). Next we arranged the air travel on a special APEX fare basis ($1,718 for two persons) and booked passage on an overnight ferry from Sweden to Finland ($207).

The rental car was $793 for 30 days, unlimited mileage. The cost for hotel rooms outside the USSR varied from $30 to $72 a night. The total for twelve nights was $577 (average $48 per night). The Soviet hotels cost $997 for nineteen nights, which is an average of $52.50 per night.

Some of the European hotels included breakfast with the room. For those that didn't, breakfast averaged $5 per person. Lunch in Europe averaged $4 per person and supper $10. None of the Soviet hotels included breakfast with the room. There, breakfast averaged $1.50 per person. A sit-down lunch averaged $3 per person and supper $5. Our daily food cost was $20 per person in Europe and $10 in the Soviet Union. We didn't eat lobster or pheasant under glass each night, but we did get some delightful meals, with wine and dessert, for that price. We often bought cheese, bread, and apple juice at a shop in the morning and had a picnic lunch at a roadside

165

park. All in all, we spent $525 for food for the month.

Gas (petrol—benzine) varied from $2.75 a gallon in Finland to $.85 a gallon in the Soviet Union. We drove 9,000 kilometers (5500 miles) and averaged 15 kilometers a liter (36 miles a gallon). The total fuel cost was $230.

While in the Soviet Union, we hired an Intourist guide in most cities and took a half-day tour of the historic sites in our car. The cost of the guide was $15. Intourist would not accept Russian currency for the tours. They want to get Western (hard) currency and happily accepted my VISA card. I'm not sure what my bank thought when the Soviet VISA charges arrived.

We spent another $400 on gifts and miscellaneous items such as bus/metro fares, exhibit entry fees, maps, and books.

The total cost of the trip was $5,742 or about $100 per person per day. With all the pleasant memories I have from the trip, I think it was a bargain.

Daily Destinations and Hotel Charges

DATE	HOTEL	CITY	COST
29 May	Flight from Dayton, OH, to Copenhagen, Denmark		
30 May	Admiral	Copenhagen, Denmark	$ 50
31 May	Hogland	Nassjo, Sweden	64
1 June	Vestervik	Vestervik, Sweden	30
2 June	Ferry from Stockholm, Sweden, to Helsinki		
3 June	Dipoli	Helsinki, Finland	42
4 June	Prebaltiskaya	Leningrad, USSR	(997)
5 June	Prebaltiskaya	Leningrad	
6 June	Intourist	Novogorod	
7 June	Tver	Kalinin	
8 June	Ukraina	Moscow	
9 June	Yaroslavl	Yaroslavl	
10 June	Ukraina	Moscow	
11 June	Galvnie Tourst Complex	Suzdal	
12 June	Galvnie Tourist Complex	Suzdal	
13 June	Shipka	Orel	
14 June	Lybed	Kiev	
15 June	Lybed	Kiev	
16 June	Octyabrskaya	Vinnitsa	
17 June	Bokovina	Chernovtsy	
18 June	Intourist	Kishinev	
19 June	Black Sea	Odessa	
20 June	Lybed	Kiev	
21 June	Mir	Rovno	
22 June	Zakarpate	Uzhgorod	
23 June	Thermal	Budapest, Hungary	$ 53
24 June	am Brillantengrung	Vennia, Austria	47
25 June	Tourist	Autobahn, Germany	35
26 June	Danhotel	Rødbyhavn, Denamrk	34
27 June	Admiral	Copenhagen, Denmark	50

28 June	Admiral	Copenhagen	50
29 June	Admiral	Copenhagen	50
30 June	Travellers	New York, NY	72

Summary of 1981 Soviet Vacation Cost

U. S. Passport fee (2 persons)	$30 (now $42 per person)
Soviet visa service	70
Traveler's checks fee	20
International driver's license	10
Hotel reservation fee	60
Air fare (2 persons)	1718
Ferry to Finland	207
Rental car	793 (30 days, unlimited mileage)
Hotel outside USSR	557 (average $48 per night)
Hotels in USSR	997 (average $52.50 per night)
Food	525
Gas	230
Tours	105
Miscellaneous	400
TOTAL	$5,742